Get Free and Stay Free

David Ohin

Get Free and Stay Free

A practical guide to identify, deliver and stay free from demonic spirits

DAVID OHIN

Get Free & Stay Free by David Ohin
Copyright © 2020 by David Ohin
All Rights Reserved.
ISBN: 978-1-59755-599-9

Published by: ADVANTAGE BOOKS™
Longwood, Florida, USA
www.advbookstore.com

This book and parts thereof may not be reproduced in any form, stored in a retrieval system or transmitted in any form by any means (electronic, mechanical, photocopy, recording or otherwise) without prior written permission of the author, except as provided by United States of America copyright law.

Scriptures quotations are taken from the NEW KING JAMES VERSION® (NKJV®). Copyright© 1982 by Thomas Nelson, Inc. Used by permission. All rights reserved.

Library of Congress Catalog Number: 2020941702

First Printing: August 2020
20 21 22 23 24 25   10 9 8 7 6 5 4 3 2 1
Printed in the United States of America

Endorsements

There is an urgent need in our day to help people receive healing & deliverance. David's handy reference book clearly lays out useful guidelines both for those receiving and those praying to restore and rescue souls from the grip of sickness & demonic problems.

This easy-to-read guide outlines general principles which most members of the Church engaging the full Gospel ministry to preach, heal, and deliver have found to be an everyday reality when praying to set captives free. This invaluable reference manual gives step by step information to those who need to see how to effectively minister & for those seeking to receive freedom in Christ. An indispensable tool for the bookshelf of any busy minister.

Rev Brian Hannant
Pastor, Gateway Community Church, Kettering, England

I have great joy in being asked to write an endorsement for David's book "Get Free and Stay Free". This short and very readable book will become a valuable weapon in any Christian's spiritual arsenal. David tackles and exposes how the spiritual realms of darkness work in order to prevent human beings from walking with Christ as their Saviour, included in His eternal victory over everything which sets itself up in rebellion and opposition to God. Exposing how they manifest and operate, what gateways they use to gain entrance into our lives, and how their hold is destroyed with the result of captives being set free; we are handed a manual or tool to help us how to take up our stand as soldiers of Christ against demons and evil spirits. There is a particularly helpful section on staying free once a demonic stronghold is broken, this is often a section which is missing from deliverance ministries. The declarations of who we are in Christ are really affirming and could be declared by all of us regularly to keep us standing firmly as children of God. David also tackles issues of healing and of course salvation. This book is written in simple terms and I feel that it is a success. I have known David for many years and have the privilege of supporting and following his ministry. David has an uncomplicated approach to ministering to the unsaved, the sick, and the spiritually bound. To Him there is no stronger Name than the Name of Jesus, and in his gentle yet authoritative way David can testify to seeing people saved, healed, and delivered. He writes from experience, holds no punches, and I'm sure you will be blessed and equipped by this book, returning time and again as you join in ministering as an ambassador of God's Kingdom.

Pastor Mark Taylor
Baptist Minister and Hospital Chaplain, England

I have very great joy in being asked to write an endorsement for David's book "Get Free & Stay Free". This short and very readable book will become a valuable weapon in any Christian's spiritual walk. Here in Africa we call David one of the gospel Ambassadors in Africa. He exposes how the spiritual realms of darkness work in order to prevent human beings from walking with Christ as their Saviour, and in His eternal victory over everything which sets itself up in rebellion and opposition to God. I see many preachers in and around the world. David is a different kind. Through his working you can see this man has God's calling and God has directed him. That is why this book can help many people around the world. This book can help to keep all of us standing firmly as children of God. David also tackles issues of healing and of course salvation in the kingdom of God.

Bishop Dr Eliah Mauza PhD
Pastor, Endtime Harvest Church
President of The Global Revival Network –Africa
East Africa Director of Proclaiming Justice to the Nations
USA Representative of AUGP (Academy Universal Global Peace)
Former secretary of Dodoma Christian Denomination Unity

Table of Contents

ENDORSEMENTS 5

FOREWORD 11

INTRODUCTION 13

CHAPTER 1: DON'T BE SCARED TO FACE THE BATTLE 15
   1 - My personal thoughts and burdens 15
   2 - On winning ground 16

CHAPTER 2: WHAT IT IS REALLY ABOUT 19
   3 - The big picture of the spiritual battle 19
   4 - Clarifying terms 21
      Oppression 21
      Depression 21
      Possession 22

CHAPTER 3: ENTRY OF EVIL SPIRITS AND DELIVERANCE 25
   5 - The overview of an effective deliverance 25
   6 - Legal grounds or footholds for demons to come in 26
      Sinful spirits (all demons are sinful) 26
      Refusal to forgive 27
      Bitterness 27
      Anger 28
      Rebellion (Prov 17:11) 28
      Abortion 28
      Intercourse 29
      Sexual sins 30
      Dirty films/pictures 30
      Drugs/Alcohol 31
      Computer games 31
      Addictions 32
      Occultic spirits 32
      Occultic organisations 32

    Occult 33
    Alternative medical practices 35
    Ancestral spirits 37
    Generational iniquity 37
    Wounding spirits 37
    Traumas/shock 37
    Rejection/hurt/abuse 38
  7 - CAN CHRISTIANS HAVE DEMONS? 39

CHAPTER 4: SOUL TIES AND CURSES 43

  8 - UNHEALTHY SOUL TIES 43
  9 - HOW TO IDENTIFY CURSES (DEUT 28) 43
  10 - CAUSES OF CURSES 44
    Verbal speech 44
    Inner vows 45
    Spiritual attack 45
    Idolatry 45
    Cursed objects 46
    Dishonouring your parents 46
    Mistreating the unfortunate 47
    Bribing 47
    Anti-Semitism 47
    Stealing and lying 47
    Striving with your Maker 47

CHAPTER 5: GETTING RID OF CURSES & EVIL SPIRITS. RECEIVING INNER HEALING . 49

  11 - HOW TO REMOVE CURSES, BREAK BONDAGES AND EXPEL ANY EVIL SPIRITS 49
  12 – INNER HEALING PROCESS 51
  13 - HOW DO YOU KNOW IF A PERSON NEEDS DELIVERANCE? 52
  14 - HOW TO MINISTER DELIVERANCE 53
  15 - DISTANCE PROXY DELIVERANCE MINISTRY 60

CHAPTER 6: HOW TO STAY FREE AND BE PROTECTED 61

  16 - HOW TO STAY FREE 61
    Lordship of Jesus 61
    Being filled with the Holy Spirit 62

- Resisting the devil 62
- Use Scripture 62
- Wear the Armour of God 67
- Counterattacks from the enemy 68
- Fellowship 69
- Mentoring / Coaching 69
- Praising & Thanking God 69
- The right company 70
- Conclusion 71
- 17 - Dealing with the primary problem 71
- 18 - How to stay protected 74

CHAPTER 7: CLEANSING CURSED LANDS, BUILDINGS ETC. 77

- 19 - Cleansing cursed lands, buildings etc 77

CHAPTER 8: PRAYING FOR HEALING 81

- 20 – Why is praying for healing important? 81
- 21 – But I am not Jesus 85
- 22 – Authority and power over sickness 86
- 23 – Two powerful tools 88
- 24 – Having faith on behalf of someone else 91
- 25 – How to pray for healing 92
- 26 – The most important aspect of the healing ministry is love 93
- 27 – We are ambassadors in this world 94
- 28 – Final words about healing 95

CHAPTER 9: FINAL WORDS 97

- 29 – Final words 97
- 30 – Conclusion 97
- 31 - Making Jesus Lord 98
  - List of occultic terms: 99
  - List of some alternative medical practices with potential danger: 100

David Ohin

Foreword

Do you feel trapped, bound or enslaved by any unwanted habits? Or have you hit a wall or an obstacle and got stuck in the process of setting somebody free? Do you suspect any demonic activities going on and you are slightly scared to tackle it? This book will equip you and give you confidence to deal with your problem. You will find out what the hindrances are and get keys which help you to attain your breakthrough. You will see how awesome the power of Jesus Christ is to set people free and destroy the work of the demonic by real life examples.

The contents of this book are applicable for both parties, the one who needs deliverance as well as the one who ministers deliverance. It's also highly beneficial for people who want to understand the nature of the warfare which goes on in our spiritual realm.

The aim is to help the ordinary person to identify footholds of the enemy in their lives and to acquire freedom and remain free. This is not meant to be an exhaustive work.

We are going to look at the big spiritual picture from the eternal perspective. What are the goals of the opposition in the spiritual battle, and how are these goals achieved? We are going to clarify biblical terms and remove misconceptions. Then we will look into the means used by demonic spirits in gaining access to a human being, and if this includes true born-again Christians too or not. We will learn how to break free from any demonic influences. We will shed light on what often happens before the demonic agents gain an advantage and the logical approach of how to prevent it. Curses on people, lands and buildings are covered too and the effect of them and how to break them. We will emphasize how to stay free and protected and also touch on inner healing. At the end we also devote a chapter to physical healing where we address some of the objections we may have. The aim is to remove the hurdles so that we can feel free to pray for the sick.

David Ohin

Introduction

A lady received acupuncture treatments every few weeks for her excruciating backache for 20 years. It wasn't possible for her to carry out a normal life without those needles as the pain was too much. We prayed for her and she was set free from evil spirits. She repented that she sought help from acupuncture (which will be explained later on in this book), gave her life to Jesus and the backache never came back. No acupuncture was needed anymore.

This doesn't make sense if it is only a physical world!

I know first-hand from a Christian man (my own dad), how the opposition put poison into his drink which would have killed him, but it had no effect on his body because he was a believer and believed Mark 16:18 *'…and if they drink anything deadly, it will by no means hurt them…'*

This doesn't make sense if it is only a physical world!

One of my friends, who was always happy, played once in his life with the ouija board and from this day forward, heavy depression set in until he repented and gave his life to Jesus.

This doesn't make sense if it is only a physical world!

I could list many more examples like this.

It is important to keep in mind that we are dealing with a spiritual dimension which cannot be understood by the natural mind.

"Now we have received, not the spirit of the world, but the Spirit who is from God, that we might know the things that have been freely given to us by God…But the natural man does not receive the things of the Spirit of God, for they are foolishness to him; nor can he know them, because they are spiritually discerned." (1 Cor 2:12-14)

There are people with a natural physical psychological problem which can be explained and treated by a psychiatrist. However, the very same problem can originate from a spiritual source, for which the same treatment has no effect. This is because the cause of the problem is different. This book is not to explain the belief in a spiritual sphere, but rather builds on that already established belief.

It's also important not to expect a demon behind every bush, (but that does not mean there aren't demons behind some bushes). The reality shows that there are more around than we think. Everyone I have met who is involved in a deliverance ministry would agree to that.

It is significant to understand the basics of the spiritual laws. The fact is that ignorance can kill you. If an ignorant child or a highly educated adult pokes a metal fork into an electric socket, then the outcome for both is the same. Ignorance doesn't prevent you from being harmed. It's exactly the same with the spiritual laws. This is the reason why it's so vital to read the book which informs us about these truths – The Bible.

CHAPTER 1

Don't be scared to face the battle

1 - My personal thoughts and burdens

It is extremely important to me to share a few personal thoughts at the outset. Unfortunately, this whole theme is a vast and very involved topic. It's not my favourite theme at all, and I wish I could have written about another subject which is more pleasant to write and read about. I didn't want to go too much into the profound stuff, but as I have come across many people who are dealing with those 'hefty' issues, I felt that for their sake, I needed to cover that too. If you are a sensitive person, I would recommend that you take what applies to you and skip what does not. My objective is to make it relevant to everybody's need. Please keep this in mind as you read on.

The second big burden I have is the fact that this is a very controversial subject in today's society. You may hear some things for the first time and a few of them may put you off or even shock you, simply because you may never have heard about it before. Please don't take this as a reason to dismiss everything else, just because you may not agree with one or two subjects or methods. There are of course different approaches and I'm not adamant about any of them. I have consulted and learnt from many different experienced people in different countries who have been involved in deliverance for a long time. From the perspective of a practical outworking of this ministry, there seems to be a general agreement to apply these principles.

However, what I DON'T want this book to be, is a recipe book! We humans love methods and formulae, but we cannot confine God and spiritual laws in a box and then think we know, have analysed, and covered everything. We mustn't think that we can turn to our recipe book and follow its directions accordingly. I hope all the information you will find in this book will be of great help to you, but there are some topics and areas I intentionally don't want to be too specific about because of the large potential for misunderstanding.

The original reason why I thought I should write something about this entire topic, was because I have seen that many cases which omit post-deliverance care, didn't stay free. If it's an occultic problem then I would even go as far as to say that without after-care, it's nearly impossible to stay free, which has been confirmed to me by someone who was originally delivered from occultic spirits. I believe that everyone who is set free will stay free when we take the after-care seriously. In many cases, I haven't seen the person anymore and I wished I could have given him or her some literature to teach them what to do next. This was my initial reason for writing this book.

We are all growing in this ministry and may not always have an immediate answer to every single question or case, but often as we start applying what we already know, God will show the next steps.

My passion is to see people set free and stay free because I thoroughly believe Jesus in His ransom on our behalf paid for this and nothing less.

2 - On winning ground

It's vital for me to set the scene correctly. Before we approach this whole topic, I want you to understand that everyone who seeks help from Jesus Christ is on winning ground. When I experienced how powerful the name of Jesus was, I was so amazed that I could never forget it. The first time I witnessed this in my own life was in Africa. I was going to preach that day and the agents in the spiritual realm knew it. On that morning around 5 am, I experienced a demonic attack. This had never happened before. Many evil spirits came in through the windows on my right side and approached me. I heard them giggling and laughing like small children. I was fully awake. This was not a dream. I could hear them as if a human being was speaking to me, or as in this case they were giggling. They attacked my mind before they reached me so that I could not think clearly anymore, and I thought I might lose consciousness. In that moment I remembered a missionary who had experienced something similar and called on the name of Jesus. I had just enough time to do that before I was knocked out or whatever else would have happened. I cried out "Jesus". When I did that, instantly every evil spirit was expelled and never came back. It was like one of the most powerful blasts imaginable! Everything was gone and the air was clear. Also, my mind was immediately and totally sound again so that I could think clearly. All of that happened within about one second. It was so fast. I was amazed at how extraordinarily powerful the name of Jesus is compared to that of the enemy. No demon can stand a chance against Jesus.

No matter how demonized you are, Jesus can set you free. Some cases may take a bit longer, but Jesus has the power to free YOU!

We don't have to fear anything! Jesus is bigger and much stronger! Evil spirits are no match for Him!

David Ohin

CHAPTER 2

What it is really about

3 - The big picture of the spiritual battle

We all agree that we are in a spiritual battle. The war is all about the souls of the human beings on planet earth. The devil wants to take as many as possible with him for eternity and he fights tirelessly for every single one with the aid of his demons which are the fallen angels who joined his rebellion against God (Isa 14:12-15; Ezek 28:12-17).

Satan knows very well that human beings are born in sin and that their only hope is to be washed from their sin by the blood of Jesus Christ and by accepting HIM as their Saviour and Lord in life. The devil knows that the more he can infiltrate a person, the more he can pull that person further away from God and make it more difficult for him to seek God for salvation. He uses well-tried methods which have proved very successful for thousands of years to tempt people into sin such as lust for wealth, sex, power or false religions and beliefs. Through all these different sins (of illusion), he can persuade you to join him in his rebellion against God. If you are enslaved by these sins *(whoever commits sin is a slave of sin* – John 8:34*)* you serve the devil unwittingly who is your master (Rom 6:16) whether you are aware of it or not. He goes as far as he can, through binding people, and tries his best to gain as much access as possible to the inner man, (soul and spirit) where he can control you in a much more powerful way. The more he can enslave you, the greater will be his success to achieve his final goals and plans for your eternity, which are to separate you from God. The devil's ultimate plan for your life, while you are still on planet earth, is that you worship him (***And he said to Him, "All these things I will give You if You will fall down and worship me."*** Matt 4:9) and to use you as a tool to destroy other lives. That's where the witches, Satanists, idolaters, murderers and thieves etc. come into play. Some are working consciously and some unconsciously for the enemy.

That's why we need to understand that a human being consists of a spirit, a soul and a body. The body is the easiest for us to understand because we can physically see and study it. Most commentators agree that the soul has three dimensions – those of the mind, the emotions and the will. These are huge topics in themselves which we will not be exploring in this book. The devil and his agents (the demons), will try to infiltrate your inner being as much as they can. Once they have gained ground to that stage, only Jesus Christ can deliver you. That's where the deliverance ministry comes in.

I will give you an example of such a victim to help you to see how an individual person fits in the big picture. One day we had a lady in our lounge who was affected by some demons after walking into a spiritualist church. We had a chat about things and the very moment we started talking about how Jesus can save her, she literally fell asleep. One moment our visitor was totally awake and the next moment she was asleep in our lounge sitting on the settee. Why? It was because the demons had made her fall asleep so that she couldn't listen to how she could be set free. We talked about other things and she was wide awake again, but the moment we switched to Jesus, the same thing happened again. If a demon has a hold on someone in that state, it's easier for the enemy to hold that person back from truly getting saved and to pursue his eternal goal for that person.

I want to describe one more experience which we had, which shows that every demonization has a single purpose and that is to stop you coming to Jesus and being saved. My wife and I were in the back garden on a skype call to someone. Our boys were playing in the pool whilst we explained to that person how he could be saved. His life was a big mess and only Jesus could help him. Then I asked him if he wanted to give his life to Jesus. Straightaway he said 'no'. He explained that he was not ready. I asked him if I could pray for him, which he accepted. I started to pray and then I switched the prayer and started to speak to the demons and bound them in Jesus' name. Afterwards, I asked the very same question again, 'Would you like to give your life to Jesus?' He said straightaway 'yes', and we led him to the LORD in prayer and he gave his life to Jesus. What was the difference between before and afterwards? The demons which literally held him back were bound and couldn't operate anymore. Demons and their activities not only make your life miserable, but they have a much bigger goal which reaches into eternity. It is extremely important to understand that God gives every human being total free will. After the demons were bound, the person was free to decide for himself. God never forces anyone to come to Him, however demons do stop a person from coming to God. As we have just seen, when demons have a hold on a person then that person can't make free choices and decisions.

4 - Clarifying terms

Before we start to look at this whole topic of freedom regarding strongholds of the enemy in your life, we need to understand the foundation of this theme. People use different terminologies and understand different meanings under different terms. If we say: "He is demon-possessed", what do we mean by it? Or "he needs deliverance!" The question then is, what does he need deliverance from?

We could split it into three main categories:

Oppression

Opression is 'suppressing in varying degrees someone's freedom and opportunities by governmental cruelty and unfairness.' This is exactly how evil spirits operate when they oppress people. Oppression is probably the mildest form of the three because it's more of an attack from outside. The word 'oppression' derives from the Latin verb, which means 'to press down'. The enemy presses you down in an area of your life. I love the verse in Acts 10:38 *'How God anointed Jesus of Nazareth with the Holy Ghost and with power: who went about doing good, and healing all that were oppressed of the devil; for God was with him.'* The Greek word for oppressed means *to exercise dominion against.* In Bible language, it means that evil spirits exercise dominion against a person. Praise God, Jesus came to free oppressed people!

Depression

Depression is 'emotional and psychological unhappiness through negative moods and feelings allowing no hope in their lives.' This can of course also be a simple chemical imbalance, but in many cases, we have found the source of the depression to be demonic. It's when demons have a hold over you in specific areas of your inner being. In this case, the demonic attack takes place within the human personality.

I remember when we were engaged in evangelism on the streets, we met a young man who suffered severely from depression. I immediately knew this was more than a chemical imbalance but rather that a demon was behind it. I prayed for him and cast the evil spirit out right there and then. Then something major happened which I have never seen before with a depression case; he stayed still for another short while and when he opened his eyes, he was a totally different person! He said he felt like he had 'woken up'. That bright shiny face told me the demon had left him. It was a work which took place in him.

Possession

Possession indicates something is owned completely. If you are demonically possessed, then you are under the control of the demon in specific areas of your life. They have a strong influence over you and can control you against your will. In that area, you have no choice but to obey the evil directive. This can range from pornography involvement to an impulse to commit murder. Prior to any demonic access to the inner human being, a legal transaction takes place consciously or unconsciously which we will look at later on. With possession, you hand over certain areas in your life to the enemy. There are many degrees of possession. You will probably rarely come across such a heavy case of demon possession as Jesus did in Luke 8:26-36; Matt 8:28-34. However, this doesn't undermine people who are possessed to a lower degree. They still need deliverance. Demons are disembodied beings and are most effective when they live out their existence and destructive works in somebody else's body. They all pursue their master's goals, who is of course satan.

The term 'demon-possession' comes from Matt 8:28; 12:22. Some versions of the Bible actually translate it 'demon-possession' whereas the Greek expression points simply to 'having a demon.' The translation 'demon-possession' can be very misleading as it gives the impression that the demon has complete control of a person. Even very strong demons are never 100 % in complete control of a person's life all of the time.

Sometimes it is not possible to clearly perceive if a person is oppressed, depressed, possessed, bound or cursed. The fact is, we are dealing with demonization and we desire the person to be free. We don't always need to understand the details of it and come to an accurate diagnosis beforehand. We should never be adamant about the above-mentioned terms because Scripture is not either. Although it sounds extremely strong, the word 'demonized' is actually more accurate in its description and includes all the varying degrees of the enemy's work and not just the extreme image that usually might come to mind, when we read or hear of the word.

So, when we talk about deliverance, then we mean to be set free of any form of demonization.

David Ohin

CHAPTER 3

Entry of evil spirits and deliverance

5 - The overview of an effective deliverance

Before we analyse the different steps and phases, I would like to lay out what the main phases are of the whole process of deliverance. This will give us a better understanding of where we are going in this, and why each phase is so significant.

1. The symptoms are what we see as evidence of the current state.
2. Prior to this is the entry point (of evil).
3. Unresolved heart issues which led to the entry point.

Usually, the work of the demons, or their activities, are just the symptoms you feel in your life. Prior to that, an entry point is created which can happen through different means, (as we shall look at later on). If we cast the evil spirit out and block the entry point, we have done well. However, even better, is to deal with the phase which takes place before the door is opened and before demonization actually occurs. In many cases, the entry point is the result of a forbidden action and that action is the consequence of an issue of the heart which has never been resolved. We could call it the primary problem. Of course, this only applies if the demonization is initiated by ourselves, which for example, excludes generational issues etc. (things which we are not the cause of and had no control over).

Prov 4:23 teaches us this fundamental truth; that all the issues we have in life spring from the heart. **'Keep your heart with all diligence, for out of it spring the issues of life.'**

We all understand that companies have, and are operated from, their headquarters. So it is with our lives. Our lives are run from the heart. So, we might describe the heart as the headquarters and centre of our lives. If things go wrong in the headquarters and wrong decisions are made, then the whole company will suffer a loss or reap unpleasant consequences. It is so in a human being's life when wrong decisions are made.

In this connection, leadership is very important. We likewise, need to find out what the influences or 'directives' of our hearts are. We need to find out who or what is influencing our thinking and behaviour, and if we need to replace those influences.

We don't want to cause an issue which leads to an entry point, that's why it's so important to guard our heart with all diligence as Proverbs teaches us to do. More about that later.

6 - Legal grounds or footholds for demons to come in

It is important to appreciate that demons are not necessarily the problem in themselves. Demons are the consequences. A feature to note in this connection is that demons are very legalistic. They recognize their right to enter into a personality as having a legal restriction. A demon can only enter a person or demonize someone if they have the right to do so. That's why it's important to remove that right so that the person stays free, which we go into later on.

There are four main categories of spirits: sinful spirits, ancestral spirits, occult spirits and wounding spirits.

Here are some doorways for demons to enter a human being under the division of the above categories:

Sinful spirits (all demons are sinful)

Yes, sin is a gateway, but please don't think that every time you sin you open the gate for a demon. It's the ongoing practice of sin that remains unconfessed and unforgiven which can result in spirits obtaining rights in some area of your life, so that they can operate and control. If you practise for example witchcraft or the Ouija board only once, then you are affected by it until you receive deliverance from Jesus.

The question we can ask at this stage is: 'Why should sin open the gateway for demonization?' We need to understand that sin is rebellion against God, that the devil started it and through it became who he is now. The judgment on him is clear and he wants everybody to join his rebellion so that they will get the same judgment. When we sin, we are not only joining satan in his rebellion against God, but also offering worship to him. When we worship satan we are making ourselves vulnerable to him and his agents the demons. Once a spirit gains access to the inner areas of a human being through a particular sin, for example, pornography, then this will enable that spirit to create pressure in the area of pornography to such a degree that the person seems unable to control it anymore. This is because the temptation occurs in a much stronger manner. In most cases, the person doesn't know that another power is active and thinks that he is responsible for these extreme urges to sin. It will put thoughts into you so that you think these are your own thoughts. This is a much more powerful way to lead you astray than attacking you from the outside. Only God can free you from it.

Refusal to forgive

It is incredible how many people struggle with this issue. The first thing we need to know is that forgiveness is the result of a choice and can also involve a process. Your main reason for coming to this place of forgiveness is simply because Jesus fully forgave you (if you truly are a born-again Christian) and therefore He desires you to forgive others also. Matt 6:14-15 clearly teaches us about this: *'For if you forgive men their trespasses, your heavenly Father will also forgive you. But if you do not forgive men their trespasses, neither will your Father forgive your trespasses.'* Jesus Himself demonstrated forgiveness in a most powerful way when He prayed: *"Father, forgive them, for they do not know what they do."* (Luke 23:34). We can pray the same as Jesus did - *'Father, forgive them ...'* because in not doing so we act like the unforgiving person in Matt 18. 23-35. Unforgiveness is a large platform for evil spirits.

Bitterness

Bitterness can easily defile us and cause a great deal of trouble, (*'Looking carefully lest anyone fall short of the grace of God; lest any root of bitterness springing up cause trouble, and by this many become defiled.'* Heb 12:15) not only in our own lives but also in others' lives. Bitterness can grow slowly or quickly and if we don't deal with it, this can become a potential doorway for the enemy to gain access.

Anger

If we persist in anger we open the door to satanic activity. Anger on the one hand can be regarded as a righteous reaction in all its various forms. An example of controlled anger is found in Mark 3:5 *('And when He had looked around at them with anger, being grieved by the hardness of their hearts, He said to the man, "Stretch out your hand." And he stretched it out, and his hand was restored as whole as the other.)* In that instructive text Jesus was said to be angry and grieved by the Pharisaical hardness of heart. Jesus' reaction can be regarded as a classical case of righteous indignation without sin.

On the other hand, the righteous indignation of us sinful mortals is likely to deteriorate rapidly into a state of sinful wrath. Thus, we are warned in Eph 4:26-27 *'Be angry, and do not sin, do not let the sun go down on your wrath, nor give place to the devil'* not to allow the sun to go down on our anger. In this connection it can be said that falling asleep in a bad mood will predictably allow the devil to exploit our anger to the full!

Rebellion (Prov 17:11)

Rebellion is a wilful resistance. Many times, it can be traced back to rejection, for example being the black sheep of the family. Rebellion is linked to witchcraft *('For rebellion is as the sin of witchcraft, and stubbornness is as iniquity and idolatry.'* 1 Sam 15:23). That's where spirits of witchcraft are operating. There is also something called 'Passive rebellion'. It's when a person resists, but doesn't show it outwardly. These people have the attitude of 'I'll do it my way' or 'I'll do it on my terms' or 'I'll do it in my time' or 'I'll do it when I feel like it.' The person doesn't feel like he rebels because he has become used to it. These are often selfish people who are not very likeable.

Abortion

One big aspect we need to consider when we look at abortion is the fact that people generally are confused about the time when a human being comes into existence. There are a lot of different opinions about it because the one who often is behind the media, (satan) wants people to believe the person you are going to kill is not really a person but just an "it", a "fetus." Once people accept that belief, they can initially kill babies without any problems. We need to appreciate that once the sperm joined the egg, we have a human being. All the different arguments by the pro-abortionists about when life starts are based on secular convenience as opposed to the reality of spiritual truth. No matter how undeveloped the person is, the spirit and the soul of the person already resides in that human being.

Many women who have aborted a baby often experienced tormenting pangs later on, which the enemy uses as a tool to condemn them. Many women struggle with terrible guilt which they never can get rid of for decades after the abortion. When the theme is flagged up, deep emotions are uncovered which drive them to dark despair.

Usually, the mother who was subject to an abortion also needs deliverance from a dominion of death because if she becomes pregnant again, the new-born child could, as a result, also be born under that dominion of death. By this I mean that the mother and the children born afterwards may have to fight against thoughts of suicides or anything related to death.

This whole topic is very sensitive! If you are in that position, then I want you to know very clearly that there is a solution for the whole act of abortion. If you repent with a sincere heart, the blood of Jesus Christ will cleanse you from every guilt, forgive your sin and justify you as if you had never had an abortion! Then you can also break the dominion of death which is behind abortion in Jesus' name. If you have already had children after the act of abortion, you (or somebody else) can pray for you and your child to break the dominion of death in Jesus' name.

Intercourse

Intercourse with anyone outside of your own marriage is clearly against God's established law. In that act, something significant is happening which we can't see in the physical realm. A spiritual link is established between both people which is called a 'soul tie'. It's not just a physical union, but also a soul and spirit union. The Bible explains it as 'two become one flesh' (Gen 2:24; Matt 19:5; Mark 10:8; 1 Cor 6:16; Eph 5:31). If this happens between a married couple then a healthy bond is established which is biblical. A husband and wife are bonding together becoming one flesh. However, if this act takes place out of wedlock then we could use the word 'a bondage' and this is created between the two, which is an unhealthy soul tie. After that spiritual transaction, demonic influence can literally be transferred to the other person. For example, if the woman had been involved with the ouija board and unintentionally was affected by a form of demonization then this can be transferred through the established channel to the man she had intercourse with. 'Bondages' and 'being bound' (in this case ungodly soul ties) always need to be broken and removed by the blood of Jesus Christ in order to be released into freedom.

Sexual sins

There are different sexual sins, like having sex with animals (bestiality) or close relatives (sister, daughter, brother, son, mother-in-law) see Deut 27:21-23; Lev 18:23. Other sins like sodomy or any kind of sexual perversion, even within marriage, can become a direct demonic entry point. Outcomes of the above can be things such as suffering from confusion about your own sexuality, being attracted to the same sex, becoming impotent or acting as the opposite sex etc.

If sexual abuse takes place, no matter how light or heavy, this can create a point of entrance for a form of demonization. Even if the victim was a young child and forgets that particular event, (which may be buried among all the other events in her or his childhood), the demons don't forget about it. It can manifest during the puberty years or even come to the surface once she or he is married resulting in great discomfort or fear of having a normal husband and wife relationship. Often it is not discovered that this is a consequence of his or her being abused as a child. You can't improve a dysfunctional sexual relationship by means of human methods like counselling etc, because the root of it is a spiritual problem. Human methods may help or give relief temporarily, but will never provide a lasting solution.

Dirty films/pictures

If you look at or watch something like pornographic material or a film on witchcraft, your eye gate is wide open and you can easily unintentionally be affected by a form of demonization that way. There are multitudes of people who became a victim by watching or looking at things. I'm not saying that when you look around and see unclean or nasty things, a demon floats into you, but when you give yourself to something and open yourself with a desire to it, that's when it gets dangerous.

Drugs/Alcohol

On top of an addiction, a form of demonization can take place too, and intensify the problem. I once heard a story of someone whose eyes were opened in a vision to the spiritual realms where he could see a demon who inserted a plug into a socket which was connected to his alcohol desire. As soon as he plugged it in, he felt that tremendous urge for alcohol. He was so shocked from the vision that he dealt with the roots of the problem and attained freedom. (I can't verify this story, but I heard it related by a godly preacher I respect very much and it matches what I believe.) God always desires us to have a sound mind and doesn't want us to be affected by drugs or alcohol and diminish our mind that way. (**'For God has not given us a spirit of fear, but of power and of love and of a sound mind.'** 2 Tim 1:7)

Computer games

This may sound strange but things like occultic games can be dangerous. If you identify yourself with a wrong, false and sinful character, then it can have power over you. It's all about the lustful imagination, which we find in Matt 5:28 **'But I say to you that whoever looks at a woman to lust for her has already committed adultery with her in his heart.'** If you identify yourself with the character and desire to be like it, or to have its power, then it can lead to sin and you can open a foothold to evil spirits in your life. I'm not saying that computer games open the doors for evil spirits, but I'm saying that certain games combined with your wilful imaginary world according to the above Scripture can definitely become a spiritual demonic entry point.

These sins are invariably linked with events. And after such an event, things can take a spiritual turn where the demonic is activated.

When you turn to the devil, for example, to become rich or successful, he will give it to you, but the price for it is always huge compared to the benefits. The majority would never want the so-called 'benefit' in the first place if they knew what the price would be afterwards. Most of the time, you don't know exactly what the price will be. It's like the small print in the contract which you agreed to when you signed it but were not aware of. This is a legal action in the spiritual world. One thing is sure, payment time always comes around.

Addictions

With any form of addiction, it is important to find out what is the root of the addiction. For example, if somebody wants to give up smoking and the cause of smoking in the first place came from being rejected, then it makes sense to look at rejection first and deal with it. There are many different causes like hatred, fear, control, abuse, sexual issues, divorce, or relationship problems etc.

Occultic spirits

These are usually more stubborn and more powerful spirits than those in the other categories, especially if people have consciously surrendered to the devil as a witch, warlock or satanist etc. Every involvement with these spirits always leads to greater and more dangerous sins. Even if at the beginning, evil spirits only lead you into smaller sins where everything may appear very harmless, they will always push you to commit worse and bigger sins. The bigger the sins, the more power they have over you.

Occultic organisations

For example, freemasons worship a god called 'Jahbulon', which incorporates the names of Baal and the fertility goddess of Egypt. Freemasonry, therefore, goes under the heading of idolatry. Idolatry is an abomination to God. The commandments warn us that the sins of the fathers in this respect will be visited upon the children for three or four generations (Ex. 20:4-5). Then Mormonism, adherents of Scientology, and other occult organisations, all fall into the same category. Even if the person has never joined such an organisation, they will be affected. The vows and curses they take in joining or participating in these things apply to themselves and their families, giving free way to demonization.

Occult

This is a very broad term. It's basically the practice of a power source which is not God. That means the source always comes from demons. The word 'occult' comes directly from the Latin word 'occultus' which means 'hidden, concealed, secret'. This is exactly how satan operates in this world. He wants to stay hidden so that nobody would realize that he actually exists. The enemy works secretly and deceives a large multitude with the occult. Once people are caught in the occult they will stay bound until the end of their lives unless they come to Jesus in a bid for freedom. Not only that, but their children will suffer consequences too (Ex. 20:5; 34:7; Num 14:18).

We are talking about things like witchcraft, yoga, black magic, white magic, sorcery, voodoo, martial arts, tarot cards, divination, consulting spirits of the dead, fortune-telling, New Age, palm reading, ouija board, astrology, angel cards etc.

I would like to mention further, New Age and yoga in this category as these have become very popular. New Age originated in the seventies and its aim is to unify the world. New Agers believe that God is all and all is God (pantheism). They believe in universalism (all religions are alternative paths to the same god and therefore all human kind will eventually be saved). This is of course the direct opposite of what the Scripture teaches (***Jesus said to him, "I am the way, the truth, and the life. No once comes to the Father except through Me." John 14:6)***. New age belief is basically an ancient occult belief updated for a modern-day practice.

The aim of practising yoga is to gain self-control, relaxation and better health through physical poses which includes mind and body. The word 'yoga' is one of the oldest words in the Hindu religion derived from the Sanskrit root 'Yuj', which means 'to join' or to 'yoke' or 'to unite'. Yoga applied leads to a union with a 'god' in a way that you will be yoked by it. You achieve this union by losing your individual identity and gain the universal one, which is exactly what the Bible warns us against. We need to be sober and not blank out our minds. Scripture teaches us in many places how important that aspect is. Here are a few:

'Be sober, be vigilant; because your adversary the devil walks about like a roaring lion, seeking whom he may devour.' (1 Pet 5:8)

'Therefore gird up the loins of your mind, be sober...' (1 Pet 1:13)

'But we have the mind of Christ.' (1 Cor 2:16)

Yoga cannot possibly be separated from its Hindu roots as you can't separate the branch from the root. It's the same tree. Yoga may appear very harmless at first sight, but if you dig deeper and do your true research you will find out that yoga is cleverly disguised demon worship and has nothing to do with the true God of the Bible.

On the contrary, the biblical meditation, which is very profitable and brings you closer to the true Almighty God of the Bible, is done by engaging the mind actively over the Word of God. If you for example take a verse of the Bible, read it through several times, pray about it, think about it and 'chew it over' in your mind, this meditation is exactly the opposite of blanking out your mind.

'Finally, brethren, whatever things are true, whatever things are noble, whatever things are just, whatever things are pure, whatever things are lovely, whatever things are of good report, if there is any virtue and if there is anything praiseworthy – meditate on these things.' (Phil 4:8)

If you want to check out some more potential dangers, at the back of the book there is a more extended list. (It is important that you understand that it is not a textbook principle that when you do this, then that is always the result. Yes, often you can tell, but it can have different effects and different levels of danger.) You only have to participate in many of these things once to become immediately demonised in an area of your life, such as using tarot cards, visiting a spiritualist or in witchcraft etc. Even participating in games just for fun like Dungeons & Dragons, table tilting or playing mirror games such as Bloody Mary and others have a great potential of danger. On the other hand, there are things which may not affect you straightaway but only when you accept it in your heart and submit to it. Then there is also a difference between practising something yourself or going to a person, or when a person comes to practise it on you. According to the spiritual law, it's basically all the same, except if someone comes to you and for example starts fortune telling over you. This happened to me once out on the streets.

You have the choice to accept or reject what the fortune teller says. If you accept it, you automatically come under his authority but if you reject it, you do not. Most of what the fortune teller tells you may be true, for example, events or current life situations. These things are very easy for evil spirits to know as they can move about on this earth and study and observe people. But then there is usually always a part which is the devil's agenda for your life. For example, he could say: "I see a car crash coming your way," or "Your marriage will fall apart," or "You will get sick" etc. If you submit in your heart to what is said over you and accept it as truth, the enemy has the legal right to bring it to pass. If you reject it, then you are safe.

Right now, I cannot make an example of every single item from the list at the back of this booklet, but if you understand the principle of it, then you can gauge for yourself where it can become dangerous. However, the strongest advice I would give you, is to stay away from it and not play with fire so that you don't get burnt.

Alternative medical practices

This topic of course also falls into the occult, but I will list it separately so that it does not get lost in the long list at the end of the book.

A woman who had a complex childhood was stricken by debilitating and chronic backache. Having rejected God and the help He could have provided, she turned instead to a crystal healer. After that she was relieved of the pain. Then characteristically the devil, who was responsible for the pains in the first place, transferred the pains to another area of her life, namely the mind. There followed a rapid mental decline. At a later stage the woman realised how her involvement in New Age practices and scientology had provided an excellent opportunity for the enemy to exploit her condition to the full. Her memory and thinking process became seriously warped so that she lost the ability to reflect clearly. It was then that God intervened on her behalf with a constructive dose of conviction. She had the good sense to repent of her sin and broke off her New Age and scientology attachment. Then the backache returned with a vengeance. Again the Lord mercifully came to her rescue with effective healing. The enemy's power was broken and the woman yielded her life to the Lord. Her backache was permanently banished and she enjoyed health and healing through a daily walk with God.

Many sick people first go and seek medical help and when that does not help, then some would seek alternative ways. If you are seriously sick or in great pain, then you are prepared to try things out which you otherwise would not even consider. Many alternative ways are totally fine, harmless and effective, but there are also many avenues which are dangerous and unsafe for your soul. They initially can look great and you could even experience bodily well-being, but the price you pay with the consequences is always much greater than the present relief you received. A very popular one is 'acupuncture'. It comes from ancient China and was practised by Taoist priests and doctors who were rooted in the pagan Taoist religion. The fact that it works doesn't make it right and safe. The dangerous part is the spiritual side effect. However, I have been made aware that there is a purely scientific practice of acupuncture which isn't connected with the spiritual realm. This method is less effective, which highlights even more the spiritual implications of acupuncture to make it 'effective'. You must bear in mind that it is not always easy to discern which is which.

Many of these alternative practitioners may be completely ignorant of the powers that lie behind the treatments they are offering. Their integrity is not in question. They mean it well and they have seen it work. I have come across many people who received bodily help from such sources and then major depression kicked in and things started to fall apart in different spheres of their lives. In other cases, a spirit of infirmity came into their life and caused many other sicknesses. Many people in this category experience inner torture and can only be set free by the blood of Jesus.

Remember how the enemy works, he has much wider objectives for your life which go into eternity.

If someone has become demonized by being healed in such a way, then decides to come to Christ and gets saved, repenting of their sin, (including that of seeking help from the devil), then the original sickness often comes back immediately and vigorously. The power of the enemy is broken and God can now do the proper healing.

With some of the healing methods you may see nothing wrong at first, but it is only when you dig deeper and do further investigation that you will find out unexpected things that you may not have known before. (Please refer to the list at the back).

Ancestral spirits

Generational iniquity

Generational iniquity can come from previous generations (Ex. 20:5; 34:7; Num 14:18). This can be already transferred in the womb. It is literally the result of a sinful lifestyle and or sinful actions of someone earlier. God is not unfair, but the sinful lifestyle is inscribed deep into the cells and genes.

We are aware of families where parents have had a particular addiction with obvious major consequences. The children hated it and did not want to end up like their parents, yet years later, they find themselves on the very same path.

I know this can seem unfair, but as we can see in our day-to-day life, we all suffer various consequences to some degree or another of other people's sinful behaviour. This is because we live in a fallen world. For example, we are all aware of situations where children are born with a disease which has been passed on from their parents. This can be regarded as a physical illustration of what can happen in the spiritual realm as well.

On the other hand, the Bible teaches us that you can pass blessings down the generations for a thousand generations *'Therefore know that the LORD your God, He is God, the faithful God who keeps covenant and mercy for a thousand generations with those who love Him and keep his commandments.' (Deut 7:9)* Also keep in mind that God always desires all to be free and saved and teaches us clearly in His Word how this can happen. God's heart is to forgive and show mercy and He wants to set us free from these consequences. This is where the deliverance ministry comes in along with inner healing which we will mention later on.

Wounding spirits

Traumas/shock

This may sound strange, but evil spirits can gain access to a human being in a situation involving a shock or traumatic event. The trauma often opens the door for the demonic to take advantage of that instant pain where humans are extremely vulnerable. That's why some people cannot let go of a particularly painful experience they had, having experienced a shocking situation. It's a bit like a physical wound. The dirt which enters the wound can cause an infection. Sometimes this can become life-threatening when it goes into the bloodstream. It's similar with psychological issues. It can start as a small emotional wound which can serve as an entrance for evil spirits, allowing them to have influence and stop the healing of the wound. Many times, traumas can even take place in the womb or in childhood. We are in a fallen world where satan is reigning and he is a very dirty fighter, exploiting every human coming under his direct influence.

If we are secure in God's love for us and wear the armour of God, then nothing can happen to us in the evil day, not even in a situation that results in trauma or shock. *'Therefore take up the whole armor of God, that you may be able to withstand in the evil day...' (Eph 6:13)*

Rejection/hurt/abuse

Many people struggle with feelings of rejection. Often people who are conceived as a supposed 'accident', struggle with a rejection obsession. Babies who survive the abortion may feel the same way. Rejection is a form of abuse. People who have been abused have very low self-esteem. All these things wouldn't make sense if there was no spiritual law and a 'spiritual' world behind it. Abuse, hurt and rejection can become a gateway for the enemy to exploit a person, causing much pain and anguish in life. Unfortunately, though it is not the fault of the person being abused, the victim can be left with need for deliverance because of the actions of the abuser.

If a mother conceives and doesn't really want the child, then she rejects the baby already in the womb. The spirit/soul of the baby can feel that rejection. It is very important to be aware of this spiritual dimension in order to understand someone's real problem. Also, on top of that, we need to be aware of the fact that when the mother rejects the child then the enemy claims the child. He knows the earlier he can establish any kind of strongholds in a child, the more difficult it will be for that person to come to Christ one day. It's important for parents to take their spiritual responsibility seriously and act as a covering for their children because the enemy always looks out for the weakest to exploit. They do that by fully accepting their children and loving them unconditionally regardless of what genders and personalities they have and bringing them up with respect and godly discipline.

This topic could be a book in itself. Many people struggle with rejection, and look at and interpret situations and people through the glasses of rejection, getting an untrue and distorted view. The root of this can often be traced to a situation where you have been hurt by someone. It may have been an intentional or unintentional act by another person, but the fact is, it hurt you. I know of a boy who, when he was approximately four, was greatly hurt by other young children his age a few times in a row. Since, then, he has built up a wall and as soon as someone tells him something in a corrective way, he feels got at and rejected. This results in a defensive reaction. It's vitally important to face the situation again and forgive those people and then ask Jesus to heal that wound. This is called inner healing. We will briefly look at that later on.

7 - Can Christians have demons?

This is where many Christians are divided in opinion. Let's ask this question in an even more pointed way: How can a Christian have the Holy Spirit and a demon at the same time? This sounds of course, totally impossible.

The problem is, that this is the wrong question. The first thing we need to examine here is, what do we actually mean by the question 'can Christians have demons'? Are demons in our spirit or in our soul, or in our body, between our soul and our body, or between our spirit and our soul? This is essential to understand, otherwise, the answer will never make sense.

It's the same as saying, 'because a Christian has the HOLY SPIRIT, he can't get sick!' The HOLY SPIRIT is Jesus' representative here on earth in power and healing etc. If HE lives in a Christian then we could rightly ask how can sickness live in that same body where the HOLY SPIRIT lives? But of course, we agree that Christians can become sick.

When you are born again the Bible teaches us clearly in 2 Cor 5:17 (*'Therefore, if anyone is in Christ, he is a new creation; old things have passed away; behold, all things have become new.'*) that you instantly will become a totally brand-new creation. The old has gone! Praise God! That is fantastic news! Before your spirit was dead (Eph 2:1; 2:5) but now you are alive. However, we mustn't forget that at the same time we have got some other rooms in a human being which need changing and renewing. They are called the will, the mind and the emotions. According to Rom 12:1-2 these rooms also need changing and transforming. This is an ongoing process and is not as instantaneous as when the spirit comes to life when we are saved, (though we long that it would be). There are also other rooms where evil spirits can hide.

If you have a demon then you have something like 'a spiritual bug' which creates a problem and a pressure in your life and this magnifies issues already there, making it difficult for you to overcome them. Evil spirits don't possess Christians. This is because your spirit is sealed with the HOLY SPIRIT for the day of redemption (Eph 1:13; 4:30). Remember that 'to be possessed' means 'to be invaded and owned'. Christians are owned by God because Jesus literally purchased us with His blood. 1 Cor 6:19-20 says:

"Or do you not know that your body is the temple of the HOLY SPIRIT who is in you, whom you have from God, and you are not your own? For you were bought at a price; therefore glorify God in your body and in your spirit, which are God's." (emphasis mine)

Jesus paid for our body, soul and spirit to belong to Himself. However, as we can let bugs and viruses into our body which Jesus had paid for, we can also let sin with its legal implications invade our soul and body too. In the same way, we say that we have a virus or a bug, we can say that we have a demon (a lodger). In other words, if we open the doorway to evil spirits, they can enter and invade an area of our lives. This means that demonic powers are in control of certain areas of our lives, which means we still want to be in charge but because the pressure is so big, we lose the upper hand and are not in charge anymore. We have lost control. If you have a house with ten rooms and you give one room to a lodger, that doesn't mean that the lodger possesses your house. It does mean that he occupies that one room and he can cause chaos in that room which is hard for you to control. You can go and tidy that room up again and again but if the lodger decides to cause further chaos, he will do it again. No matter how many times you tidy up after the lodger causes a mess, you have an ongoing problem because the lodger's personality is untidy. The only way you can solve the problem is to throw the lodger out. So, we can put it this way, a Christian's spirit can't be taken over by evil spirits, but he can still be demonized in other areas of his life. I have come across many clearly born-again Christians who were transformed by the power of God but had one or two issues in their life which they couldn't control because somebody else was in control. These evil spirits usually present from the days before they accepted Christ as their Saviour or are inherited through previous generations. Sometimes the demons get weaker once the person comes to Christ, but usually, do not leave voluntarily. They still need casting out. With this conclusion, we can safely say that some Christians still need deliverance in vulnerable areas of their lives.

Sometimes you can have as much counselling and encouragement as you want, but you will still struggle with a certain issue, because there is a demonic power behind it which prevents you from gaining the victory and it needs to be expelled and dealt with.

David Ohin

CHAPTER 4

Soul ties and curses

8 - Unhealthy soul ties

Unhealthy soul ties can also be established without sexual sins, for example in a parent-child relationship. The key to understanding if it's a healthy or an unhealthy soul tie lies in discerning whether you can live with a free will according to the Bible or if you are bound to other people or their opinions in any way. This can even happen between a pastor and a Christian from his congregation.

I once met a woman who simply couldn't break free from her abusing partner. In the natural that doesn't make sense to anyone, but spiritually it makes perfect sense. It's because an unhealthy soul tie was established between them. When you break these unhealthy soul ties between two people in Jesus name then a spiritual transaction takes place immediately. Sometimes the other person can feel it straightaway.

You can even be soul tied to a dead person. That's when you just can't ever let them go. You suffer so much more than you should. Then there are soul ties to idols, pornographic images or even between a tattoo and tattooist.

9 - How to identify curses (Deut 28)

The first thing we need to be aware of is, if there is a curse, then there must be a cause.

When we talk about curses, then we are looking for repeated patterns, including chronic diseases. For example, if someone repeatedly suffers breakdowns, including a marital breakdown in the family line, then that can be identified as a curse. Also, if a person is continually suicidal, if a person experiences continual financial setbacks no matter how hard they try to succeed or if a woman keeps having miscarriages, that often is linked to a curse. Also if a person is prone to accidents or is like a magnet to sicknesses and illnesses, then we may also be able to reach the same conclusion.

I know someone who had seven car accidents. You can imagine after the first few he drove so carefully and yet it seemed he couldn't be prevented from further accidents. After a while he realised he was intentionally cursed by someone. After these curses were broken, he stayed accident free.

10 - Causes of curses

It is important to understand that curses are not imposed by God. He did however establish the spiritual laws which are right and just. If we go against them, we hurt ourselves. For example, if we go through a red traffic light, we can crash. If we put our hand on the hot stove, we burn ourselves. If we jump down from a bridge, we could be severely harmed. If we lie too long in the sun, we get sunburnt. God didn't actively put any of these consequences on me. Therefore, I can't blame God for it. It's very similar when we look at curses.

There are many different causes of curses. Here are just a few:

Verbal speech

Many times they are spoken out intentionally or unintentionally. I know of someone who hated her parents and verbalised with an intense wish that they would have a painful chronic disease and that's exactly what happened for both of them. We need to keep in mind the reality of Prov 18:21 **'Death and life are in the power of the tongue'**. Our speech is very powerful! We can use our tongue to curse or to bless people. This principle also applies to ourselves as much as to others. Many people curse themselves, for example by saying "I'm rubbish", or "The world would be better off without me", or "I will never achieve anything in life". Another way powerful curses are spoken out is when parents or teachers say to children things like: "You are silly", or "You can't do anything right", or "You will never make it to anything in life", or "You are just a problem and a burden". I have personally seen adults who were greatly affected by such negative prophecies spoken out by parents and teachers when they were young. Some of them experienced exactly what was said over them because they believed it and lived up to it. In many cases, the victims have a self-complex or even have a suicidal tendency. They have believed and accepted the words spoken over them and the curse has been realised in their lives.

On a more encouraging note, I'm pleased to point out that we can use the same principle to bless, strengthen and build up people by speaking out life and blessings over them.

Inner vows

This is a form of self-curse. It often originates in a horrible life situation that you never want to experience again and you made up your mind to protect yourself from repeating such incidents in your life. Following that, an inner vow is established, saying to yourself things like:

"All who are close to me have hurt me, I will never let anyone get close to me again!"

"I have failed so many times, I would be better off dead!"

"I will never forgive myself for this huge blunder I have caused!"

"I will never marry, all men are wicked!"

Spiritual attack

This occurs when a witch or a Satanist places a curse on you. There are always evil spirits involved when this happens. This is very common in Africa. However, the same takes place in Europe but it is less obvious. The biggest difference is that the majority of the people in Africa are familiar with it and in Europe, they are not. I could write a book giving examples of demonic attacks and curses, not only about that which I have heard and seen, but also of God's miraculous and supernatural protection from such attempts, even where angels were involved among very close relatives in my family.

Idolatry

The Bible often teaches that idolatry can also bring a curse on a person (Deut 27:15; 29:18-20). With that curse, sickness often, if not always, comes with it. Idolatry can be practised in many different ways. It's not only to worship a statue or the sun etc. but it also covers placing a buddha in your lounge or anything else you would hope to help or protect you.

Cursed objects

Objects which have been cursed or used for witchcraft make a huge demonic impact, especially when you have them in your home. It not only makes the atmosphere cold and dull, but it can literally be used for evil spirits to impact your life with problems such as a whole series of sicknesses or financial loss or destroying your marriage etc. Sometimes it can be a lucky charm or an idol you buy in a shop like a buddha or inherited jewellery etc.

Dishonouring your parents

This one may sound strange, but makes very much sense when we read Eph 6:2-3 *'Honour your father and mother, which is the first commandment with promise: that it may be well with you and you may live long on the earth.'* The result of honouring your parents is 'prosperity in life and living longer'. That implies that 'not honouring your parents' can result in it not being well with you or even a shortened life (premature death).

In this case you need to deal with the root issue of your disposition toward your parents. All parents have flaws and make mistakes. Ask God clearly to help you to forgive your parents and to be able to love and appreciate them. After all, if they weren't here, you wouldn't be either. You need to discover the heart of the problem. Did they hurt you, upset you or disappoint you? Try to look at them through the eyes of Jesus and forgive them.

How do you know if you have an issue with your parents? One indication is if you get agitated in their presence or if you can't stand their mannerisms. Another sign is when you feel tension if they are around or even if you are thinking of them. The result of these feelings can be a tendency to treat them with contempt. Deut 27:16 says *'Cursed is the one who treats his father or his mother with contempt.'* Some people struggle greatly with their parents, blaming God for giving them such difficult and odd parents. We need to let God be God and accept the way He made our parents. They have their faults like the rest of us and God can change them too. They also have been created in the image of God as all humans have been *('So God created man in His own image; in the image of God He created him; male and female He created them.'* Gen 1:27*)* If we believe Rom 8:28 *'And we know that all things work together for good to those who love God, to those who are the* *called according to His purpose'* then we are convinced that God can grant us blessing in our lives even through difficult parents.

Mistreating the unfortunate

You can add a curse by exploiting or ill-treating the blind, fatherless, widows, handicapped, disabled, poor and the unfortunate. (Deut 27:18-19). God is a just and compassionate God and wants to protect the unfortunate. There are countless Scriptures which indicate that God cares very much for disadvantaged and vulnerable people.

Bribing

'Cursed is the one who takes a bribe to slay an innocent person' (Deut 27:25). Many people have killed or wanted to kill others because of a bribe. We have experienced that a few times in the family, but thankfully God stopped it supernaturally. However, if the impulse is allowed to continue, the conscience pangs can torment that person for life.

Anti-Semitism

Any negative action or words against Jews can bring a curse on you *('I will bless those who bless you, and I will curse him who curses you…'* Gen 12:3). The Bible teaches us that he who touches the Jews, touches the apple of God's eye (Zech 2:8). Here I can only say, you don't want to trifle with God's eye!

Stealing and lying

Often stealing and lying go together. Stealing is the first action and lying is the cover up of the action. According to Zech 5:3-4 thieves can bring a curse on themselves, as well as perjurers (people who swear falsely/make wrong statements under an oath about someone by lying).

Striving with your Maker

'Woe to him who strives with his Maker! Let the potsherd strive with the potsherds of the earth!

Shall the clay say to him who forms it, what are you making? Or shall your handiwork say, 'He has no hands?' (Isa 45:9)

This covers a lot of areas in our lives. Many things we don't like about ourselves such as our character or our body can build up in the back of our mind and we can blame God. After a while, you may end up thinking that it's His fault that you are the way you are. Then other people may enforce these issues in your life by agreeing with you or speaking out negative words. In the end, you reject the truth about what God really thinks of you, which is clearly revealed in Psa 139:14. You will not be able to agree with God and say **'I will praise You, for I am fearfully and wonderfully made; marvellous are Your works, and that my soul knows very well.'** Yes, God will change you more and more into His likeness, and sanctify you, but in His eyes you are already regarded as His workmanship.

CHAPTER 5

Getting rid of curses and evil spirits and receiving inner healing

11 - How to remove curses, break bondages and expel any evil spirits present in the personality

When we remove a curse then we remove the legal rights for demons to have access to a particular area in your life (Gal 3:13-14). We should never be adamant about any method as God doesn't bind us to methods. It is extremely important to engage your heart fully in each of these steps and not run it through in a mechanical way. I would like to give you a few possible guidelines on how to remove curses, break bondages and cast out evil spirits effectively. Technically you can do that on your own, however it is always much easier if a born-again Christian does it with you and accompanies you in the process.

1) Admit and face the problem/sin

The first step is vital, yet many undermine it. It's simple to recognise, acknowledge and face the problem or the sin. You need to own the problem and admit it. Don't make excuses and shift the problem or sin by blaming other people for it. For example, saying: "I have this struggle in life because of the way my parents brought me up." This is not owning and admitting, but shifting the problem by blaming your parents.

2) Repent

Come to the Lord and thank Him for the mighty victory He accomplished on the cross to deal with any sins and destructive works of the devil, including the breaking of curses. Then repent of all curse-related sins which give the right for the curse to be there. If you have stolen, repent of it and pay it back if possible. If you cherished an idol, repent and get rid of it and remove the root of it. Ask God for forgiveness and cleansing.

3) Release forgiveness
If you suffer the consequences of somebody else putting a curse on you, then forgive that person for Christ's sake. Speak it out loud and release the person into forgiveness (Matt 18:21-35). If you feel you must forgive anyone else, especially if it's related to your demonic problem, then do that now. Then if you need to forgive yourself, speak it out loud.

4) Renunciation
If it's a curse issue, then renounce the curse over your life and separate yourself from it. Renounce the wrong identity you have taken on and declare the new identity.

5) Cast out
Now is the time to take authority over the evil spirit(s) and address it with authority. You speak directly to the evil spirit(s) saying something like: "In the name of Jesus Christ, I command you to leave now. Go in Jesus' name and never come back…" You don't need to shout, but you say it firmly with authority as one who really means it (because you do mean it). You do this with an attitude of expectancy that it will go.

6) Receive
Many times after demonic powers have left or ceased their operation, the person feels relieved but also empty or sometimes even weird. This is because that agent is not there anymore. That's why it's very important at this point in time to ask God to fill you with His HOLY SPIRIT and the peace of God. You just receive His filling by faith and He will do it in a constructive way.

7) Resist

In the spiritual realms you have now decided that you have submitted to God's authority and laws and want to live for Him. From now on, you will keep resisting the enemy in your mind but also verbally if he wants to render a visit again in the future. You are now practising James 4:7 *'Therefore submit to God. Resist the devil and he will flee from you.'*

12 – Inner healing process

When a person needs inner healing, for example, if someone suffers the consequences of a trauma or a shock, then your primary focus is on inner healing. Always be very tender-hearted with the victim. You pray for the person, taking the victim back to the painful experience and asking God to heal the wounds. It's always helpful if you let the person express in prayer his or her acceptance of God's healing. Inner healing has nothing to do with removing the memory but takes the sting out of the experience.

It's always helpful to ask the Holy Spirit to bring up any childhood memories, especially the hurting ones. Then you ask the person if he/she would allow you to pray through that situation. We can ask Jesus to come to these memories so that He can deal with them for us.

We can do that because we know clearly from Scripture that Jesus is omnipresent and was there when it happened. Ask them to verbally voice out their desire for Jesus to come.

This is only a process where the person lets Jesus into their memory and emotions to heal them. Encourage them to receive by faith the love and healing of Jesus. It is important to ask the person if they would forgive the perpetrator with the Holy Spirit's help. It may be necessary, if for example it was a case of being abused when young, that they may need to hear that the experience wasn't their fault. Clarify to them that the perpetrator would have to give an account of themself to Jesus for what they had done. Forgiving them is not equal to justifying them and saying it's ok what they did. It is in effect handing vengeance and justice completely over to the Lord to work out. Adults often feel guilty and ashamed because they can't reconcile themselves with who they were as a child because of what had happened to them then.

The above scenario is just an example how it can be done. We should never be adamant about using a particular method. However, this is meant as a support for those who let themselves be led by the HOLY SPIRIT. The main issue is that Jesus needs to come into the situation and heal the inner wounds.

Some people don't need any of the above or similar scenarios as they have enough faith to reach out to Jesus to heal their inner pain without even going back to the trauma. It's not a method, it's a person – JESUS! It's not our prayers. It's not our know how. It's not our experiences. It's JESUS CHRIST only!

Once the wound is healed you can command the evil spirit which attached itself to that wound to go and never come back. After that ask God to fill the person with His love and peace, as most cases go back to a lack of love, affection and affirmation.

13 - How do you know if a person needs deliverance?

1. The obvious one is when the person tells you so. Often people know something is wrong with them and can sense that this is a spiritual issue.

2. I often found when I prayed for people with laying on of hands, that while I prayed, a bodily reaction started to take place and then I knew the person needed deliverance. When the HOLY SPIRIT who is in you comes in touch with demonic forces, a reaction may then take place. There are many different reactions like shaking, twitching, acting strangely, going for the throat, a demon starting to speak to you (for example, saying "we are not leaving"), a woman starting to speak with a man's voice, changes in facial expression, eyes rolling back so that you can only see the white element (the demon doesn't want to look into your eyes as you represent Christ), parts of the body go rigid, eyes go glassy, the

person arches their spine backward, rolling on the ground or acting like an animal etc.

3. If you get to know about the person's history, then sometimes you can confidently conclude that one plus one equals two, and a demon, or more than one, is hiding somewhere in that person. From most of the occultic involvements, no-one gets away without some form of demonization.

14 - How to minister deliverance

Basically, all born-again Christians have the power in Christ to pray for demonized people and set them free. However, I would like to give a few guidelines.

1. It's always best to have someone else with you when you carry out a deliverance ministry.

2. It's important to discern if the person really needs deliverance or if the need is actually inner healing.

3. You need to find out by an interview, or the gift of discernment, what kind of spirit you are dealing with. Ask questions, like, "when did it start?" "How long have you struggled with the issue?" "What did you do beforehand?" "What happened?" When the person, for example, says: "My mother died just before I got suicidal", you may then suspect that there is a spirit of death in operation or an unhealthy soul tie.

4. Deliverance has a lot to do with knowing your secure place in Christ. The demons notice straightaway who has authority and who hasn't. The fact is if you are a born-again Christian you have authority, but you may not believe it. If you don't believe it yourself then be assured the demons won't believe it either. The following verse assures us that Jesus Himself gave us authority and that we are fully protected from the enemy too. Luke 10:19 ***"Behold, I give you the authority to trample on***

serpents and scorpions, and over all the power of the enemy, and nothing shall by any means hurt you."

5. If you have doubts, then I recommend that you protect yourself, your whole family and anyone who is involved, with the blood of Jesus Christ before you start the deliverance session.

6. If you live in conscious sin and you want to minister deliverance to someone, I would recommend that you sort yourself out first; repent and put things right before God.

7. Before you start the deliverance ministry, a time of worship can provide a real incentive declaring that HE is King of kings and that all things are under his authority etc. This is very powerful and changes the spiritual atmosphere immediately. You can pray in tongues too and your spirit will be strengthened straight-away as it is stated in Jude 20 "*...**building yourself up on your most holy faith, praying in the Holy Spirit.***" I remember once when I prayed to set someone free, I started to lift up the name of Jesus Christ for maybe 30 seconds and someone else saw me in a vision how my spiritual muscles were growing fast in that time. It was a very easy deliverance which didn't take long at all. It's a very simple but powerful tool.

8. This is now a good moment for the person to commit his life to Jesus and make HIM Lord of his life. If the person made an act of surrender to the devil, like becoming a witch, warlock, satanist etc. then the person needs to clearly repent and commit his/her life to Jesus and state that they want to leave satan's kingdom, otherwise it's most likely that they will not be able to do so. When they come to the essential part in the prayer, they may not be able to say 'Jesus Christ' or the very sentence where they hand their life over to Jesus. In that case, you would need to bind the resisting spirits and command them to stop interfering. Then let the person pray again. Once they are able to say it, let them declare it several times to the spiritual world that they want to serve JESUS CHRIST for the rest of their lives.

9. Evil spirits of this category need to be renounced, which is basically not just confessing and repenting but clearly and actively turning against it. I highly advise involving a team or somebody well experienced in the deliverance ministry when you are dealing with heavy occultic cases. These are powerful demons that are confronting you. If the person or his ancestors made any covenant like a blood covenant or a word covenant with the devil, the victim needs to clearly renounce the involvement. Blood covenants with the enemy are extremely powerful. If repentance is required then note the following suggested guideline:

"I confess and repent on behalf of my ancestors/specific name(s)/priests of satan etc. for all animal and human sacrifices they have made…"

After that, the revocation of the covenants are very important:
    a. "I renounce in the name of Jesus Christ, every covenant and blood covenant that my ancestors have made within areas of witchcraft, open satanism, freemasonry, sorcery…"

    b. "I renounce any consecration and rituals, including sexual rituals, and disempower everything in Jesus' name."

    c. "I renounce any occult calling over my life in Jesus' name. Jesus, I ask you now, through your blood, to make ineffective any ritual involving blood sacrifice in my life."

    d. "I renounce and make ineffective over my life any satanic worship, sacrifices, tongues, gifts, teachings, prophecies, ancestral blood scripts etc."

After that, you can cast out all the occultic spirits and close the gates of entry, (you can also anoint the person with oil on the forehead).

You can now proclaim the truth and power of the blood covenant of Jesus Christ.

Of course, along with that, all satanic emblems, books, tarot cards, any written contracts etc. need to be thrown out of the house or even better, be burnt in Jesus' name (Acts 19:19). Whenever we conduct a crusade in Africa, we make a public fire for all witchcraft and satanic items to be burnt.

10. One of the most powerful ways, if not THE most powerful way to disarm evil spirits, is the believer's water baptism. After people have committed their lives to Jesus and they are baptised in water, all evil spirits will lose their grip on the person's life. After that, the deliverance is always much easier. I have seen demons manifesting immediately and leave when they came up from the water.

11. If a person has many evil spirits, it doesn't do any harm to have different sessions over a course of days or weeks and cast out one or a few at once. However, if you have the energy and the time, then why not complete the job in one session?

12. Don't shout at the demons. They are not deaf. Your authority doesn't lie in the volume of your voice, but in Jesus Christ. Give an authoritative command.

13. Don't slap or push the demonized person! The slapping or pushing doesn't get the demon out.

14. In Jesus' Name you can also forbid the evil spirits who are in the person to draw power from any other spirits from outside of the person. That sometimes can make the session a bit easier. The kingdom of darkness is also organised in hierarchy. Sometimes higher and more powerful demons can strengthen weaker and less ranked evil spirits from the outside. Somebody I have ministered to in deliverance experienced that scenario in a very powerful way.

15. Looking the person in the eyes can be very helpful. The eyes are like a mirror of the soul. Often you can see if there is anger, hatred, mockery, pride or unforgiveness etc. deep down by looking into their eyes. Also, demons normally can't stand you looking into the eyes, because it's a power confrontation. When Jesus lives in you, the demons can see Him in you. Sometimes the eyes roll back so that you can only see the whites

because they want to avoid looking into your eyes. In this case, you can command the spirits to look into your eyes.

16. Sometimes in a deliverance session the spirit takes over the person's voice when you address it. You will notice straightaway when the demon takes over. In that moment, the actual person you are ministering to is out of it and will have no recollection of what is happening. By no means feel offended in any way by what the evil spirit may speak to you, as you know it's not the person talking to you but the demon.

    We had once a case where the person had two different demons and you could see when his personality was taken over by demon one and when demon two was in control. You also could see clearly when the demons went dormant again and the man came back to his awareness and was his real self. Observe intently what is happening during a deliverance session and you can understand much better what is going on.

17. Some argue that if you touch, (lay hands on) the person then the evil spirit can enter into you. However, I have experienced the contrary. I firmly believe that I'm protected (Luke 10:19). When the power of the Holy Spirit (Who is in me) and the demon come together by touch, then a reaction will take place. I often have seen in that moment, a manifestation occurs which can be all sorts of things. When the demon surfaces you can cast it out. However, I would recommend that if you are unsure about whether to lay hands on the demonized person, then I recommend you not to do it. It can be dangerous if you lay hands on the person doubting that the demon could attack you. In the end, it all comes down to your faith. Both ways are right. I personally practise both approaches. Quite often I lay hands on the person and pray until the demon surfaces and then I take my hands off and cast it out verbally stretching my right hand towards the person and motion the demon to come out. Basically, using my hand to support my authoritative verbal command to the demon.

18. You never ask God to send the evil spirit away, because Jesus gave you the order to cast it out (***"Heal the sick, cleanse the lepers, raise the dead, cast out demons. Freely you have received, freely give."*** Matt 10:8). You speak directly to the demon with an authoritative voice saying something like, "*In the name of Jesus Christ I command you evil spirit (if you know the name or the activity of it then you can name it) to go and never come back.*" You can also add something like, "*leave quietly and without any disturbance.*"

19. Sometimes it can be a long battle. Here I need to very clearly highlight that it's not about who is stronger! It's not a power battle. It's about the position you take in Christ. I had once a case in Uganda which lasted approximately forty-five minutes. It was very hot, I was tired and hungry but I kept going by the grace of God. I couldn't postpone the deliverance because we were travelling back home the next day. I asked "How many of you are in her?" They answered: "We are many". I knew I was dealing with stubborn witchcraft spirits. They had indwelt a twelve-year-old girl. After forty-five minutes they all left. I don't like postponing deliverance sessions, but sometimes if the circumstances force you to, then don't feel guilty, as long as you do it later on, or on another day. I have heard of cases lasting hours.

Why did that case with the girl in Uganda take that long? I had a few hindrances to overcome which could have been dealt with much more easily if I had more time and could speak the language. If the situation had allowed me to talk the girl through forgiving her offender, renouncing a few things and tackle the inner healing, then the whole process of deliverance would have proved much easier. So, I went for the next best and omitted the above first steps and chose the direct confrontation with the enemy immediately.

20. Sometimes you can shorten the session if you involve the person who needs deliverance as much as possible in the process. For example, to let the person repeat what you are saying: "In the name of Jesus Christ I command you, evil spirit of anger to leave now" etc. Or, involve them in

renouncing the work of the enemy in their life. Or simply to declare with an act of will that "Jesus is my Lord and I want to serve Him only and not an evil spirit." Sometimes the demon will not allow the afflicted person to say these things. In that case, you who are ministering should just carry on as it's not a necessity.

21. If the evil spirit hasn't taken over the individual's personality, then ask the person to whom you are ministering pointed questions, like "What is going on?" or "What do you feel?" etc. Often, they then answer with things like "I feel something moving in my stomach" or "I feel a tremendous sadness coming over me." This helps you to assess what stage you are at in the battle because these are all emotions and activities of the demon and not of the person.

22. How do you know if the evil spirit or spirits have left?
The easiest way, of course, is if you have the gift of discernment. But even if you don't have that gift, you can still know. Look very closely at the person's face. When you see the person's eyes suddenly become normal again like those of a normal human being without the glassy cold eyes, or whatever facial expression the demon displayed, then you know it has gone. In other cases, it is when the violent demonstrations cease. If somebody coughs or vomits, keep commanding the evil spirit until the person stops coughing or vomiting. When the person is fully conscious and the demon doesn't take over the individual's personality, then you can ask the person if it has gone. Often, the person knows. Be very careful, when the person you minister to says, I feel better and lighter. That doesn't necessarily mean that all have gone. It can also mean that maybe one of a number of evil spirits have left. Just reassure by asking again if the person still feels there is something there. But sometimes it's obvious and the person feels totally free, light and relieved instantly. Praying and listening to the Holy Spirit is the most important thing you can do during a deliverance session.

23. Sometimes you may need to be aware of your surroundings. I once prayed for a pastor's wife that she might be healed, after a normal church

service in the area where people mingle for tea and coffee, and then I noticed that the source of the pain was demonic. I had to stop as the demon started to manifest and I was aware that I was dealing with the pastor's wife. It's better to treat some cases in a more private environment.

24. After a deliverance session always ask God to fill any empty space as the person will be in a spiritual vacuum and will be feeling totally empty. Deliverance is like spiritual surgery. It's as if you cut off a major part of a person. Let the peace of God enter and saturate the person completely.

When you have finished the deliverance ministry, you can also pray for yourself and all the people who were involved in it and for their families to be protected and filled with the Holy Spirit etc.

15 - Distance proxy deliverance ministry

We read the story of the Syro-Phoenician woman who came to Jesus on behalf of her demonized daughter who was absent that time (Matt 15:21-28; Mark 7:24-30). In this proxy deliverance, we need to pay attention to one or two things. Yes, it is possible to cast out demons at a distance as distance is not a hindrance in the spiritual realms. However, we need to point out in this story that the daughter's mother legally was the daughter's cover as she was still a child. The mother had the right as her spiritual protective cover to make that decision for her daughter. This is a definite yes scenario so go for it. If the daughter was an adult in her own right and might not want to get free (which would be unusual), then you may not succeed in this deliverance. Having pointed out these aspects I still wouldn't want to draw a concrete conclusion of when to carry out such a proxy deliverance or when not.

CHAPTER 6

How to stay free and be protected

16 - How to stay free

When an unclean spirit goes out of a man, he goes through dry places, seeking rest, and finds none. Then he says, 'I will return to my house from which I came.' And when he comes, he finds it empty, swept, and put in order. Then he goes and takes with him seven other spirits more wicked than himself, and they enter and dwell there; and the last state of that man is worse than the first. So shall it also be with this wicked generation. (Matt 12:43-45)

I would like to remind you of the big picture. We are in a huge war. The enemy doesn't give up quickly. He bows his knees before Jesus Christ and leaves the human being when he is cast out, but he seeks to come back to regain the territory which he lost. I would like to point out a few things you can do to protect yourself from the enemy coming back to regain your territory. These are all basic things (but very powerful) and should be normal in a Christian's life.

Lordship of Jesus

It is essential that you hand over your lordship to Jesus the King of kings. He has purchased you with His blood and you belong to Him (Acts 20:28). This applies of course only if you are a born-again Christian. If Jesus is Lord of every room in your (human being) house, then it's impossible for the enemy to come back and reign because the King of kings is already reigning in the house.

Being filled with the Holy Spirit

This leads me to my next point. Eph 5:18 commands us to be continuously filled with the Holy Spirit. It's pretty straightforward. When the Holy Spirit occupies every room in your life then there is no space for the enemy to come back. Simply ask the Holy Spirit to indwell you and fill every single room of your life (Luke 11:9-13).

Resisting the devil

If you have submitted to the Lordship of Jesus Christ and the Holy Spirit dwells in you, then James 4:7 instructs us to resist the devil. With 'resisting' I don't mean to push back slightly when the enemy is trying to gain access via your door. What I do mean is to get all pumped up inside of you and carry out acts of violence (in the spirit) kicking the enemy with force, so that he realises you are serious about not wanting him to come back. You fight with the same intensity as in a war. You can also use words like "Evil spirit, I command you, leave. I don't want anything to do with you. The King of kings lives in me now and I serve Him alone, go in Jesus' name!" You say these words with conviction and authority. If your words come from the heart then they are extremely powerful in the spiritual world! Another approach is to totally ignore the enemy by paying no attention to him as you have surrendered your life already whole-heartedly to Christ. This is also a powerful form of resistance (silent resistance). You will soon discover that the enemy will flee after that according to James 4:7 *'Therefore submit to God. Resist the devil and he will flee from you.'*

Use Scripture

Of course, the Word of God is a Christian's spiritual nutrition which should be absorbed daily. If you don't eat for a few days then your body gets very weak. You would even find it difficult to move about and fighting in a war is simply impossible if you have no strength. It's the very same in our spiritual life. Now I would suggest that on top of your daily reading, you look up verses which apply specifically to your situation. Meditate on these verses. Chew them over and express them. It depends what the initial foothold was which enabled the enemy to gain access to your life. If it was through rejection, anger, sexual sins etc. then you should find Scripture which deals with that topic. After having meditated and chewed it over you can make it into a daily prayer or proclamation.

For example:

(Material from 'God's Unbreakable Word to You', produced 1994 by Fred Elgar. Used with permission of Mrs Barbara Elgar.)

(Past action by God which continues to be effective for me today)

- *"I have been delivered from the dominion of darkness and transferred into the kingdom of God's Son." Col 1:13*
- *"I have been ransomed by the precious blood of Christ from the futile way of life inherited from my forefathers." 1 Pet 1:18-19*
- *"I have been set free from the curse of the law of sin and death." Rom 8:2 / Gal 3:13*
- *"I have been reconciled to God by Jesus Christ." 2 Cor 5:18 / Rom 5:11 / Col 1:22*
- *"I have been saved by God's grace, by faith." Eph 2:8*
- *"I have been born again of imperishable seed." 1 Pet 1:23*
- *"I have become a participator in the divine nature." 2 Pet 1:4*
- *"I have eternal life." 1 John 5:11 / John 5:24 / John 6:47*
- *"I have been qualified to share in the inheritance of the saints." Col 1:12*
- *"God has poured His love into my heart by the Holy Spirit He has given me." Rom 5:5*
- *"I have received His righteousness." Rom 4:23-24 / 2 Cor 5:21 / Phil 3:9*
- *"I have put on Christ because I have been baptised in Christ." Gal 3:27*
- *"I have been crucified with Christ." Gal 2:20*
- *"I have been buried with Christ through baptism." Rom 6:4 / Col 2:12*
- *"I have been made alive with Christ." Eph 2:5 / Col 2:13*
- *"I have been raised up with Christ and am seated with Him in the heavenly place." Eph 2:6 / Col 3:1*

- *"My life is hidden with Christ in God." Col 3:3*
- *"I have been sealed in Him with the promised Holy Spirit." Eph 1:13*
- *"I have been blessed by God with every spiritual blessing in Christ." Eph 1:3*
- *"I have been justified by faith and by the blood of Jesus and by His grace." Rom 5:1 / Rom 5:9 / Rom 3:24*
- *"I have been washed, sanctified, justified in the name of the Lord Jesus Christ and by the Holy Spirit." 1 Cor 6:11 / Rom 5:1*
- *"God chose me in Christ before the creation of the world." Eph 1:4*
- *"I have been called according to His purpose." Rom 8:28*

(My present status and value to God is because:)

- *"I am a new creation." 2 Cor 5:17*
- *"I am united to the Lord and am one spirit with Him." 1 Cor 6:17*
- *"I am in Christ." 1 Cor 1:30 / Eph 1:3*
- *"I am holy and blameless in God's sight because I am in Christ." Eph 1:4*
- *"I have been brought near by the blood of Christ." Eph 2:13*
- *"I have the mind of Christ." 1 Cor 2:16*
- *"My body is a temple of the Holy Spirit." 1 Cor 6:19*
- *"I am a child of God through faith in Jesus Christ." Rom 8:14-16 / Gal 3:26*
- *"I am a joint heir with Christ." Rom 8:17*
- *"I am holy and dearly loved because God has chosen me." Col 3:12*
- *"I am a member of God's household." Eph 2:19*
- *"I am one of the people who belong to God." 1Pet 2:9*
- *"I am one of His chosen people." 1 Pet 2:9*
- *"I am a fellow-citizen with the saints, part of the holy nation." Eph 2:19 / 1 Pet2:9*
- *"I belong to the Royal priesthood." 1 Pet 2:9*

- *"I am being transformed and conformed into the likeness of Jesus Christ." Rom 8:29 / 2 Cor 3:18*
- *"I am a light in the world." Mat 5:14*
- *"I am the salt of the earth." Mat 5:13*
- *"I am an ambassador for Christ." 2 Cor 5:20*

(Because of these things, it is therefore true of me that:)

- *"I can understand what God has freely given me." 1 Cor 2:12*
- *"I can know God's will and have all spiritual wisdom and understanding." Col 1:9*
- *"I can be filled with the Holy Spirit." Eph 5:18*
- *"I can live a life worthy of the Lord." Col 1:10*
- *"I can please the Lord in every way." Col 1:10*
- *"I can grow in the knowledge of God." Col 1:10*
- *"I can continue to live in Christ and be strengthened in faith." Col 2:6-7*
- *"I can be more than a conqueror through Him who loves me." Rom 8:37*
- *"I can count myself dead to sin." Rom 6:11*
- *"I can overcome Satan by the blood of the Lamb and the word of my testimony." Rev 12:11*
- *"I can overcome the world." 1 Joh 5:4-5*
- *"I can inherit the promises through faith and patience." Heb 6:12*
- *"I can approach the throne of grace with confidence." Heb 4:16*
- *"I can have confidence to enter the most Holy Place by the blood of Jesus." Heb 10:19*
- *"I have access to the Father by the Holy Spirit." Eph 2:18*
- *"I can draw near to God with a sincere heart and full assurance of faith." Heb 10:22*
- *"I can be holy in all my conduct because He who called me is holy." 1 Pet 1:15*
- *"I can take every thought captive to make it obedient to Christ." 2 Cor 10:5*

- *"I can be transformed by the renewing of my mind."* Rom 12:2
- *"I can do everything God asks me to with the help of Christ who give me the strength and power."* Phil 4:13
- *"I can have my heart guarded by the peace of God."* Phil 4:7
- *"There is now no condemnation for me because I am in Christ Jesus."* Rom 8:1

(God will continually do for me that which I cannot do for myself:)

- *"He will work in all things for my good because I love Him and have been called according to His purpose."* Rom 8:28
- *"He will be with me always, to the very end of the age."* Matt 28:20
- *"He will keep me strong to the end so that I shall be blameless when Jesus Christ returns."* 1 Cor 1:8 / Jude 24
- *"The good work He has begun in me He will carry on to completion."* Phil 1:6
- *"He will not allow anything to separate me from His love."* Rom 8:39
- *"He will meet all my needs."* Phil 4:19
- *"He will not allow me to be tempted beyond what I can bear, but will provide a way of escape."* 1 Cor 10:13
- *"He is able to keep me from falling."* Jude 24
- *"He has prepared in advance good works for me to do."* Eph 2:10
- *"He will answer my prayer when I ask in Jesus' name."* John 16:23-24
- *"He always lives to intercede for me."* Heb 7:25

(Copyright held by Ellel Ministries Pierrepont.)
Use these Scriptures like vitamin supplements on top of your meal.

Once after a deliverance session I conducted over the phone, one of my prayer team members saw a vision of an empty cow's stomach. It referred to the spiritual situation of the person I ministered to. It signified that there was no spiritual food in the stomach. The Holy Spirit pointed out, that it was now extremely important to 'eat' the Scripture and 'chew it over' multiple times until the stomach was full. A cow actually has four stomachs. This is a beautiful picture of meditating on Scripture (to break down the food multiple times). After the digestion takes place, abundant fresh milk will be the result of it. With that milk, the rest of their household will be able to be spiritually fed too.

This is a very important part which is clearly taught in Phil 4:8-9

('Finally, brethren, whatever things are true, whatever things are noble, whatever things are just, whatever things are pure, whatever things are lovely, whatever things are of good report, if there is any virtue and if there is anything praiseworthy – meditate on these things. The things which you learned and received and heard and saw in me, these do, and the God of peace will be with you.')

The enemy will assault your mind so that you will dwell on those negative thoughts and the whole original problem becomes alive again before your eyes and will be blown out of proportion. The moment you are accepting that as a truth, demons can manipulate the foothold again. Whereas, if you do the opposite and dwell on the truth directly from the Word of God, then you put iron locks onto your doors and it will be extra safe.

Wear the Armour of God

Study every single weapon in Eph 6:10-18 carefully and use these weapons actively against the enemy. Meditate and think which weapon you are most likely to need to use in your case. There will be no doubt *'above all, taking the shield of faith with which you will be able to quench all the fiery darts of the wicked one.'* Eph 6:16 will have to be used a lot, as the enemy will fire lies at you. If you accept his lies then he could eventually get in again. For example, if the enemy tells you: "Still nobody likes you. Nothing has changed since the deliverance. You should still feel hurt inside of you and have self-pity because the people you have forgiven still are against you and will hurt you again and your Lord won't help you. Therefore, you have the right to be upset again and feel rejected." If you don't use the shield of faith and if you accept the lie, then you hold these words above the words of the Lord Jesus and therefore Jesus isn't the Lord anymore in that specific area. Consequently, the enemy may have an opportunity to lord over you again in that part of your life and gain access. However, if you use the shield of faith by saying: "I have chosen to completely forgive them, even though they still hate me, because God forgave me too according to Luke 6:37 **'Forgive, and you will be forgiven'**. I choose not to be hurt and rejected but trust that my Lord will help me because I believe Heb 13:6 *'The LORD is my helper, I will not fear. What can man do to me?'* You can also choose not to receive the hurt and choose to leave it for the Lord to deal with.

Here some more examples how you can use the sword of the Spirit and the shield of faith:

Enemy: Too many tragedies have taken place in your life!

You: *But God is faithful, who will not allow you to be tempted beyond what you are able* (1 Cor 10:13).

Enemy: Your whole faith business is a lie and nonsense!

You: God is not a man, that He should lie (Num 23:19).

Enemy: God doesn't really love you!

You: *God is love* (1 John 4:16). *For God so loved the world that He gave His only begotten Son, that whoever believes in Him should not perish but have everlasting life* (John 3:16).

Enemy: You can't trust God and the Bible!

You: *Blessed are all those who put their trust in Him* (Psa 2:12).

Enemy: God can't even help you!

You: *Is anything too hard for the LORD?* (Gen 18:14).

Enemy: He is not interested in your life!

You: *He makes my way perfect* (2 Sam 22:33).

Counterattacks from the enemy

Be on your guard in the area where the enemy came into your life in the first place. The devil will place temptations before you, especially in that area where a specific sin was the port of entry. Ask others to pray for you and help you. That's why it's extremely important that the source of the problem/weakness which in many cases originated in the heart is dealt with or given special attention for protection.

Another common attack is when the demons come back to harass you, trying to convince you that they are operating in you again as in previous times. However, the fact is, that they are fighting you from the outside wanting to come in. The moment you agree and believe they are inside you, the door opens and they have won that battle.

Then some demons are excellent talkers and try to open a discussion with you. Never even start that! You expel them ruthlessly and immediately in Jesus' name.

Fellowship

This leads me to my next point. If you are in fellowship (1 Cor 1:9 / 1 John 1:7) with other Christians and you ask others to support you and help you, then you will not feel on your own in your battle, especially after your deliverance. Two or three soldiers are stronger than one.

Mentoring / Coaching

This is in addition to fellowship. It's vitally important if you could find a mature Christian with whom you can share your progress and struggles. No doubt there will be questions that will arise and you need to be able to ask someone who you can trust. This is the easiest way to grow and become stronger. It would be the ideal situation if you could find someone.

Praising & Thanking God

When Jesus healed the ten lepers only one came back to thank Him. What about the other nine lepers? Did they already forget the Healer? I think nowadays we have got about the same percentage. If it goes well 10% may give thanks and praise to Him. Here I want to draw your attention to Jesus having taken notice of the one leper who came back saying: *"Were there not ten cleansed? But where are the nine?"* (Luke 17:17) Jesus, knowing that thankfulness is for our own benefit and for God's glorification, pointed out the heart issue in the next verse where we read: *"Were there not any found who returned to give glory to God except this foreigner?"* Jesus points out clearly that when we thank Him, we glorify Him. I think it's only right to thank Him, especially if He has just delivered us from the hands of the enemy.

Praising is also one of the most effective tools against depression and a heavy spirit. Isa 61:3 says: *'The garment of praise for the spirit of heaviness.'*

The New Testament only speaks of three sacrifices, which are expected from us:

1. In Rom 12:1 to give our bodies as a living sacrifice.

2. In Heb 13:16 *'But do not forget to do good and to share, for with such sacrifices God is well pleased.'*

3. And in Heb 13:15 *'Therefore by Him let us continually offer the sacrifice of praise to God, that is, the fruit of our lips, giving thanks to His name.'*

Note, a sacrifice normally doesn't grow naturally. Sometimes we need to endeavour to bring a Praise sacrifice which can go against our feelings. It is much easier to bring our request catalogue to God than to praise Him.

Praising God is very powerful in the spiritual world. It changes the atmosphere and the enemy doesn't feel comfortable in it. If you praise Him, you draw close to Him and as a result, the enemy can't stand it. James 4:8 says: *"Draw near to God and He will draw near to you."* If God is near to you then it's much easier to overcome temptations and fight the enemy!

Somebody I cast out a few demons from, told me that when she walks the dog, (which is where the demons come near her again, wanting to come back in), she praises God. As soon as she starts to praise God and sing to Him the demons leave her straightaway.

The right company

It's very important to be in the right company. 1 Cor 15:33 teaches us very clearly, saying: *'Do not be deceived: Evil company corrupts good habits.'* It's like if you have a bowl of fruit, good and bad fruit. The good fruit doesn't make the bad fruit good, but the bad fruit makes the good fruit bad. We can't take this illustration one to one, but we need to be very much aware of the fact that if we mingle with the wrong crowd we can easily slip into sin and bad habits. This is even more of a problem if those wrong people have helped you to open up to the enemy in the first place.

Conclusion

Overall, it's basically doing what we read in Rom 12:2 **'and do not be conformed to this world, but be transformed by the renewing of your mind.'** I cannot emphasize enough that adapting to the way of how God is thinking is the best protection from anything coming back. This applies particularly in the area of where the roots of the problems originated from. For example, if a spirit of rejection came in while the victim was still innocently in the womb, and that person gets delivered as an adult, then he/she needs to pay particular attention to renewing the mind in the area of rejection. In practice that can look like this: if that person concerned is totally ignored in a situation where it normally would hurt emotionally, then he/she person needs to make a choice. Either the individual will accept and invite the pain of rejection back or instead says, "I'm loved by Jesus and I'm not rejected. This situation cannot hurt me." What happened here? The person decided to renew the mind by adopting to act out the truth of the Word of God, rather than how he/she felt. Once the pattern of this is adjusted to the Word of God and the mind is renewed in that area, then there is no possibility for any spirit of rejection to come back. It's like when a heavy smoker changes his lifestyle and eats healthily instead of smoking after his cancer was removed successfully, then the risk of getting the lung cancer back is greatly eliminated. In this whole process, we fully rely on God and His help.

17 - Dealing with the primary problem

'Keep your heart with all diligence, for out of it spring the issues of life.' (Prov 4:23)

The issues of life come from the heart. The heart is the centre of our being. Everything comes from the heart. If something is wrong in our life then it can be traced back to an issue which went wrong in the heart. That's the place where the primary problem is created.

We could look at our heart as our house. We have different rooms. In each room, something can go wrong. If something goes wrong, we can attract unwanted visitors and problems. For example, if we leave our fruit bowl in the kitchen too long in the heat, some of the fruit goes off. After a few days, it gets rotten and not long afterwards you see fruit flies around the bowl and in the whole kitchen. The most effective way to combat the fruit flies is to remove the bad fruit first. This is the original cause of the unwanted visitors. Once the cause is removed, it's easy to deal with the invaders. It's exactly the same with demons. Once the cause of the attractions for demons is removed, it's easy to cast them out so that they stay out. The demons are only the secondary problem. If we deal first with the primary problem, (which is the issues of the heart) the demons won't come back. Rotten fruit and fruit flies go together. It's the same in the spiritual laws.

There are different approaches on how to minister inner healing. In the end, only Jesus can heal the person inside. Some would do it as following in practice:

Let's say a man called Frank is battling big time with anger. Frank has lived with anger nearly all his life and therefore opened the door to the spirit of anger which intensifies the emotions even more and makes it impossible for Frank to control it. It's as if the DNA changed and Frank is hopelessly exposed to uncontrollable anger. It's great if you cast the demon of anger out of Frank, but it's much greater if you can find out where and why the original problem of anger started in the heart. The real issue, which is the primary problem, is in the heart. After a few questions you discover that when Frank was twelve years old, his dad walked out and left mum. In that moment the anger started to grow against his dad and then developed against everyone else. Now we need to deal with the issue of the heart. There are two major transactions which need to take place, inner healing and forgiveness. Talk to Frank who is thirty-five years old, but take him back in his memory to that point in time and speak to that 'twelve-year-old boy'. Ask him how he felt when his dad walked out. Confront him with the pain. I know that may sound difficult and cruel, but remember the wound needs to be uncovered and bare before God can heal it (just like a physical wound needs to be exposed and cleaned before it can be healed). Maybe a few tears will drop down and emotions will get very intense. Then gently invite Frank to recognize Jesus the loving God was right there with him in that very painful situation. He was not alone! We know that, because the Bible teaches us that God is omnipresent. He cared for him all these years. Invite Frank to give all these hurts and pains to Jesus. This is so important that he gives them to Him because we cannot progress to healing if we keep hold of them. Invite him to receive by faith healing from Jesus. Then ask him if he is able to forgive his dad with the help of the Holy Spirit? Maybe you need to further explain to him that forgiveness is not a feeling but an act of the will and also that it is not saying that the behaviour was acceptable. After Frank has forgiven his dad, you address the spirit of anger and cast it out in the name of Jesus, which is usually an easy transaction after the primary problem has been dealt with. Now you have not just removed the fruit flies, but the bad fruit too which was the primary issue.

This is just an example. There are hundreds of different scenarios, but the same principle. It is important also to know that God is not bound to a certain way to heal a person on the inside. The only thing which probably stays the same is the person needing to face the pain first, acknowledging it and letting it be uncovered and giving it to Him. This process is so important because it is handing the situation over to Jesus for Him to deal with. In effect it is acknowledging god is to judge that person not me. Some people may find it helpful to do this by thinking 'that situation and or person is on God's 'To Do List' now, not mine.' Or 'It's in God's 'In Tray', so I can leave it with Him.' It can help to know 'it will be dealt with, but just not by me, but by God'. Once they have come to the conclusion that it wasn't God who caused it, you ask Jesus to heal the person. You can't expect a wound to heal or go away immediately. You need to address it to ensure healing.

We need to do everything possible to keep our hearts because that's the place where things start going wrong.

Sometimes we need to break habits and patterns of life which can be extremely hard and involving a fierce battle. That includes retraining our muscle memory (automatic action). For example, if we use the following analogy: I love cakes, chocolate and ice cream, fatty cheeses and yogurts and most of the stuff which is bad for you. When I used to go to a shop, I always gravitated automatically to these products. I developed a muscle memory, meaning if I didn't have a specific purpose for what I needed to buy, then I found myself standing in front of products like that before I was even aware of what I was doing! My feet were programmed to take me to these products. I have meanwhile changed my whole food lifestyle which took me years. I now think differently. At the beginning it was hard, but now it's so much easier because my habits have changed and therefore so has my muscle memory. I still enjoy these products, but they do not have the hold any more that they used to have. In fact, some of it I don't really eat any more.

Many times, with God's help, we need to change a few life habits in order to maintain the victory more easily.

In conclusion, we always need to see the wider picture. We don't only want to cut the tree to a stump, but we want to do a proper job and uproot the tree with its roots.

18 - How to stay protected

Ultimately it all comes down to knowing who you are in Christ (if you are a born-again Christian). If you know and believe that you are a son or a daughter of the Almighty God and you walk in His ways then nothing can touch you. Luke 10:19 says: **'Behold, I give you the authority to trample on serpents and scorpions, and over all the power of the enemy, and nothing shall by any means hurt you.'** 'Nothing' means nothing in every language! If we believe this, accept and apply this truth to our own life, we have the most powerful protection there is on planet earth backed up by God Himself.

For example, many people tried to kill my Dad (who is a missionary in Africa) for years in multiple ways by witchcraft and with other physical tools like poison, knife etc. Literally, nothing worked. In each attempt, the poison didn't affect him *('...if they drink anything deadly, it will by no means hurt them...'* Mark 16:18). On one occasion, when a murderer was on the way to perform his act, he had an accident on the way and literally died before he could kill my Dad. On another occasion, the arm with the knife in the person's hand froze. Dozens and dozens of witchcraft attempts failed because the One who is on our side is so much bigger and stronger than the enemy. We need to hide in Him and make Him our shield (Psa 91). Another time, when demons were literally sent to destroy, an angel was behind my Dad and protected him. I was literally there in that room where it happened. I could tell many more stories, but the most important lesson to learn here is the fact that when we believe Luke 10:19 then this verse can become the most powerful shield there is in the spiritual realms. There is also another very powerful verse regarding protection from curses in Prov 26:2 **'Like a flitting sparrow, like a flying swallow, so a curse without cause shall not alight.'** That means if you believe that no curse can touch you and you don't give any rights to the enemy (by any way we looked at above) and someone places a curse against you then that curse will never be activated. Your faith in Jesus literally will protect you from any spiritual attacks.

Another very powerful way, and it is very easy to do, is to simply protect your house. When we freed a woman from many demons, they still came in and out of her house as they pleased. I instructed her to protect the house in Jesus' name. To go to the door and windows of the house and seal it with the blood of Jesus by saying something like: *"In the name of Jesus from now on no evil spirit can come into this door/window anymore. I seal every entry into this house with the blood of Jesus Christ. Every spirit which wants to come in by visitors will stay outside. I block every entrance to any dark powers in Jesus' name".*

After that things immediately became quiet in her house.

David Ohin

CHAPTER 7

Cleansing cursed lands, buildings etc.

19 - Cleansing cursed lands, buildings etc

This may sound strange for some people, but land, properties, objects and organisations can actually be cursed too. Curses can be placed on buildings by witches, warlocks etc. even from generations past. I know of a Christian man who stayed over-night in a hotel. One room in that hotel was distinctly spooky. Every guest reported to the reception in the morning how scary the night was. They gave my Christian friend that room but he didn't know anything about its reputation. He protected the room in Jesus' name (as he usually does) and in the morning the people at the reception asked him how the night had been. They were very surprised when he said that he had slept well. The power of the blood of Jesus Christ is much stronger than any curses and powers of the darkness.

We were dealing with a case where everything went wrong in the house. The atmosphere was cold and depressing. Problem after problem was the norm. We knew immediately that we were dealing with a curse. The Lord revealed to us that a witch was involved and had buried an occultic letter with curses on it at the front door of the house. When we started to pray about it, the spiritual world got alerted and the witches became disturbed. We broke the curse on the house and annulled the buried occultic letter with a prayer. That can be done from any distance, as distance doesn't matter in the spiritual realms (we were hundreds of miles away). The Lord revealed a few more things which we dealt with, and in the end, we consecrated the whole house and family to the Lord. The depression was instantly lifted and the atmosphere dramatically changed from that very moment onward. All the powers of the darkness were expelled in one moment.

In situations where active witchcraft attacks are going on, it is very important after the house is cleansed and free to protect it on a daily basis with the blood of Jesus Christ. This needs to be done especially to the house doors and windows of the home. Occultic demons, witches, warlocks etc. are very stubborn and don't quit that quickly. However, there is nothing to worry about as we are on the winning side with Jesus, but we need to apply His blood and use the protection He has provided for us in this active spiritual warfare in which we are engaged.

There is a way by which you can cleanse lands, buildings etc.:

1. It's always good to have the legal owner of it with you or have his/her consent to cleanse the land and break the curses. If they don't agree, you still can go ahead and bind the dark powers though you may be limited in the process. Like my friend noted above was unaffected by the curse, it did not mean however that the curse was fully removed from that hotel room.

2. Find out what has happened to the property in the past. Was there any practice of occultism, masonic links, violence, sexual activities, criminal activity etc.? Put things right where you need to and are able to do so.

3. Choose to forgive the people who initiated these sins or were part of it or caused the curses and spells over your property. Speak it out loudly that you have fully forgiven them. The spiritual world is very much aware of what is going on.

4. As the legal owner confesses these sins very specifically, mentioning them by name and repenting of them, forgiveness can be assumed and the whole issue dealt with. If these sins have been committed by others, then you confess and repent on their behalf.

5. You declare now with reference to the heavenly realm that you have legal and spiritual authority in the Name of Jesus over all the powers of darkness over your building. Then you break the curses, spells and any demonic operation with an authoritative voice in Jesus' name. Set the building free in Jesus' name and command the dark powers to go and never come back. Make sure you include the surrounding of the building and everything that legally belongs to it. Depending on the situation you can do that in every single room and by walking around

on the land, carrying out this act of authority, or you can do it generally, maybe touching the corner of the building.

6. Then consecrate the building fully to God. If you so desire, you can even anoint the four corners with oil and pray over it. Pray God's presence down into your building and ask the Holy Spirit to fill every single room belonging to it. Declare that you have made Jesus King over your building and that you submit it to His authority.

7. Then protect the whole building in Jesus' name. Seal it with the blood of Jesus Christ and ensure an effective defence against any demonic powers.

8. Sometimes God unfolds the state of the building in a step by step process so that the whole process can't be done in one moment. Be sensitive to the Holy Spirit and ask God to expose the truth and be obedient by acting according to what HE is showing you.

David Ohin

CHAPTER 8

Praying for Healing

20 – Why is praying for healing important?

Often divine healing is in conjunction with deliverance and may need to be focused afterwards. To my surprise I have discovered that many pains and sicknesses originate from a demonic source. That means that the condition will often disappear straightaway after the person has been set free from any demonization. However, in some cases demons leave but the pain or sickness stays. There are two explanations for this. One is that the root cause wasn't demonic but a normal sickness or a pain totally separate from any demonic influence. Secondly, the cause was demonic but for some reason the pain or the sickness stayed. In either way it is important to pray for healing.

I have seen many healings, even deaf ears opening up after decades of being deaf, but I have also seen many who weren't healed. I'm by no means where I would like to be and there is still much room for me to grow. However, I would like to share a few thoughts to inspire you and to help you to grow into a natural way to pray for people's healing.

The first issue which we need to settle is that God is equally interested in healing as well as effecting deliverance. My aim is to show you that God's heart is to heal. There are many different hurdles people have in the form of objections which keep them away from believing and praying for healing. My intention is now to remove as many objections as you may have in your mind so that you will feel free in your spirit and heart to pray in faith.

Once you know if healing is the will of God it will be so much easier to pray for people. Often, we shy away from praying for healing simply because we are not sure if it's in God's will to heal that person. This thought already reduces our level of faith to a huge extent. When we analyse this issue more carefully, we have to look for good arguments which would support the thinking that God maybe doesn't want to heal this person. In the end we are looking for biblical proof either for or against the belief that God wants to heal.

Let's come up with the most powerful arguments I have come across; those who say it's not God's will to heal. In this connection they speak about 'my experience'. This maybe the strongest argument. They say, in 'my experience' God hasn't always engaged in healing. It is far removed from verses like:

> **'Then Jesus went about all the cities and villages, teaching in their synagogues, preaching the gospel of the kingdom, and healing <u>every sickness</u> and <u>every disease</u> among the people.' (Matt 9:35) (emphasis mine)**

This simply shows us that Jesus literally dealt with every sickness and disease. 'My experience' falls far short of this. In this moment of comparison something happens immediately. The level of faith drops right down to rock bottom. Why did my faith decrease drastically when the Word of God is meant to increase my faith? Rom 10:17 teaches us: **'So then faith comes by hearing, and hearing by the word of God.'** The instant before your faith failed, you unconsciously made two decisions.

1. You believed the Word of God. That was the correct decision.
2. After that you didn't hear what the Word of God was saying to you personally, but instead you were paying attention to the wrong voice. That voice came from that person inside of you called 'My Experience'. The trouble was that voice was so loud that you were not able anymore to hear what the Word of God was saying. You accepted it as truth and the result of it was immediate confusion and your faith evaporated.

You have put your experience above the Word of God and therefore your voice of experience was much louder and became your reality once again.

The question is now, how can we make the voice of the 'Word of God' louder than the voice of 'My Experience'? The most important ingredient in this recipe is: **Make the decision to believe God's Word more than what**

you have experienced so far in your life. I remember many years ago when I had a bad stomach ache. I was about to get into my car. I had hardly prayed for other people at that stage and decided to start with my own body. I stayed in the position where the stomach ache hurt the most and laid my hands on my stomach. I made the decision not to believe that loud voice from My Experience. I prayed something like this: In the name of Jesus Christ I command you stomach ache LEAVE! In Jesus' name GO! I kept praying in a similar way like that and consciously paid much attention to the Scripture *'by his stripes we are healed'* (Isa 53:5). The voice of My Experience started to fade away and the power of Isaiah 53 namely *'by his stripes we are healed'* became louder. At the same time, I noticed that my stomach pain was rapidly diminishing. I carried on and the pain left. My faith shot up and I felt happy and victorious.

What exactly had happened? The shift of attention from My Experience changed to the Word of God. It started by my conscious decision to honour the Word of God more than my own experience. By doing that I realised how *'faith comes by hearing'*. I could suddenly hear the Bible louder than My Experience. As a result of that I could experience what the Word of God was saying in the first place.

I believe that this is a good strategy to promote development in faith until **'healing 'every sickness and every disease'** will become our new reality. I still feel I'm miles away from this, but the more I silence My Experience the more the biblical reality becomes my own reality. It's all about which plumb line of reality we decide to go by.

Another strong argument is 'My Own Belief'. This sounds very odd at first. Of course, everybody has got their own beliefs! Is this wrong? The answer is simple. If your own belief doesn't match the Bible, then it's wrong. Our belief is extremely powerful. People have done the most crazy things imaginable because they believed in something. We act by what we believe. We do that without thinking. We open the refrigerator because we believe there is something in it. We go to work because we believe at the end of the month we will get paid. Many actions we carry out can be traced back to what we believe. Belief has a strong influence when it comes to healing too. The reason for that is, you have already built up a belief system of your own doctrine of healing by what you have heard in the past and have been influenced by other people around you. What you have read about in the past has shaped your belief system. Basically, your source of information formulated your own belief which is either biblical or unbiblical.

Let's look at a biblical incident:

'And when the men of that place recognized Him, they sent out into all that surrounding region, brought to Him all who were sick, and begged Him that they might only touch the hem of His garment. And as many as touched it were made perfectly well.' (Matt 14:35-36) (emphasis mine)

Why did these people touch Jesus' garment? Because they simply believed if they did, they would be healed. What made them believe that in the first place? What was the history of belief in the doctrine of healing? What made them so sure that if they touched Jesus' garment, they would be healed? There were most likely two groups of people. The first group believed, because they simply saw what had happened to the person who received his/her healing before their eyes. The second group consists of those who have never seen it before. However, they may have heard about it from others beforehand. With this we come back again to the Scripture ***'So then faith comes by hearing, and hearing by the word of God.'*** (Rom 10:17) It literally came from the Word of God. Do I mean they have read it in the Bible first? Not necessarily! They heard it from the lips of Jesus directly and we read in John 1:14 that Jesus is the Word of God.

If My Own Belief says you can only be healed if all your sin has been dealt with, then this belief could be your hindrance to receiving healing. The fact is we don't read that Jesus ever responded in that way. If My Own Belief screams loudly with a religious voice "It's not the will of God for you to be healed because God needs this sickness to shape your character first" then your Belief is likely to have blocked your faith. The truth however is that Jesus never answered in that way. He never said 'this sickness serves for you to become more holy'. This was only the voice of My Belief. We read:

'And the whole multitude sought to touch Him, for power went out from Him and healed them all.' (Luke 6:19) (emphasis mine)

'But when the multitudes knew it, they followed Him; and He received them and spoke to them about the kingdom of God, and <u>healed those who had need of healing.</u>' (Luke 9:11)

Maybe it's time to challenge everything else that My Own Belief is proclaiming and see if Jesus agrees?

21 – But I am not Jesus

You may say now that this sounds all so good and wonderful, but the fact is 'I'm not Jesus'! We need to answer this essential part of the doctrine of healing as it is one of the foundation stones without which the whole building could collapse later on.

We know that Jesus healed everyone who came to Him and didn't reject one single person. We also know that Jesus carried out 100% of the will of the Father, including healing and deliverance. In John 6:38 Jesus says ***"For I have come down from heaven, not to do My will, but the will of Him who sent Me."*** This confirms to us that it was also the Father's will for everybody to receive their healing. We could say now: "But Jesus was 100% human and 100% God while He was on earth! Does that very fact not make the whole difference? He was 100% God and we are not!" Let's analyse this argument. Are we actually saying that "God hesitates to heal everybody through us but He didn't through Jesus because Jesus was God and we are not?" The Father's heart is still disposed to heal. Jesus has sent us to do exactly the same (Matt 10:8). His heart was to heal too as He was united with the Father's heart. The question is, has Jesus changed His mind 2000 years later or not? We know from Heb 13:8 *'**Jesus Christ, is the same yesterday, today, and forever'*** that Jesus hasn't changed His mind. This gives us confidence that He wants to address the sick people in the same way today as He did 2000 years ago. Anything else wouldn't line up with the heart of God.

Let's look at another significant verse in Acts 10:38 *'**How God anointed Jesus of Nazareth with the Holy Spirit and with power, who went about doing good and healing all who were oppressed by the devil, <u>for God was with Him</u>.'*** **(emphasis mine)** It doesn't say Jesus healed all because He was God (even though He was and still is God). It says Jesus healed all <u>because</u>

God was with Him. And because God is with you and me too, we can do the same, as He promised us in Matt 28:20 '*I am with you <u>always</u>, even to the end of the age.*' God anointed Jesus to do these works and Jesus anoints every single born-again Christian too as we read in 1 John 2:27 '*But the anointing which you have received from Him abides in you.*' It is clear that Jesus wants us to walk on this earth as He walked in every aspect of life. This is how He is glorified the most and not through sickness. Here are some powerful Scriptures which emphasize this truth:

> '*By this we know that we are in Him. He who says he abides in Him <u>ought himself also to walk just as He walked.</u>*' *(1 John 2:6 (emphasis mine)*

> '*Love has been perfected among us in this: that we may have boldness in the day of judgment; <u>because as He is, so are we in this world.</u>*' *(1 John 4:17) (emphasis mine)*

> '*Most assuredly, I say to you, he who believes in Me, the works that I do <u>he will do also</u>; and greater works than these <u>he will do</u>, because I go to My Father. And whatever you ask in My name, that I will do, that the Father may be glorified in the Son.*' *(John 14:12-13) (emphasis mine)*

Be encouraged and pray that the Holy Spirit will change you more and more into the likeness of Jesus Christ in every area of life!

22 – Authority and power over sickness

As we have established some essential aspects in the last two chapters I want to expand a bit more on another key element. We need to understand the authority Jesus Himself has given us. We read in Luke 9:1 '*Then He called His twelve disciples together and gave them power and authority over all demons, <u>and to cure diseases.</u>*' However, the last part of the verse clearly states that we have the same authority to cure diseases too. In other words, we are given authority over sicknesses and diseases. But notice too, it is acting under authority to do it, for it is simply carrying out Jesus' command, just as the centurion said, '*For I also am a man under authority, having soldiers under me.*' Matt 8:9. A king has authority. When he gives a command then it's usually carried out according to his wishes. If people decide to rebel against it then the king can enforce his law by military force. Usually the authority he has is enough, but sometimes he uses an extra means namely 'military power'. The biblical terminology is 'exousia' (authority) and 'dunamis' (power). We read in Luke 10:19 ***'Behold, I give you the <u>authority (exousia)</u> to trample on serpents and scorpions, and over all the <u>power (dunamis)</u> of the enemy...' (emphasis mine)*** I have witnessed instant and gradual healings over the phone. How did that happen? It happened by authority only, because I spoke to the pain or sickness to go. If that doesn't work then God has provided us with a second means called power (dunamis). This is when you touch the sickness (the sick person), for example by the laying on of hands. The Holy Spirit dwells in you and therefore you are filled with His power. As a result the power flows out of you and destroys the pain or sickness. Here are a few scriptural examples:

> *'Wherever He entered, into villages, cities, or the country, they laid the sick in the marketplaces, and begged Him that they might just touch the hem of His garment. And <u>as many as touched Him were made well.</u>' (Mark 6:56) (emphasis mine)*

> *'...came from behind and touched the border of His garment. And immediately her flow of blood stopped.' (Luke 8:44)*

> *'And the whole multitude sought to <u>touch Him</u>, for <u>power</u> (dunamis) <u>went out from Him</u> and healed them all.' (Luke 6:19) (emphasis mine)*

We find another powerful verse in Rom 8:11 where the above truths are in evidence:

> *'But if the Spirit of Him who raised Jesus from the dead <u>dwells in you</u>, He who raised Christ from the dead will also <u>give life to your mortal bodies</u> through His Spirit who dwells in you.' (Romans 8:11) (emphasis mine)*

The Holy Spirit who empowered Jesus will empower you also. If distance is involved you are limited to authority only and if you are with the person you have both means available.

Whenever you express authority, it is vital to know that you actually possess the authority. If you give out the same command to a country like a king does, then nothing will happen, because you don't have the king's authority. If you step into a company and give an order to every employee, nothing will happen, because you are not in charge of the company. You lack the authority, because you were not given the authority over the country or company. Secondly, your voice would sound very unsure and wimpish when you give that command or order, because you are aware that you have no say in the country or company. However, when it comes to healing you have a lot to say, because Jesus Himself has given you authority over sickness and directed you to carry it out ('**Heal the sick, cleanse the lepers, raise the dead, cast out demons. Freely you have received, freely give.**' Matt 10:8) It's a command from Jesus and he has given you the authority freely. We can pray with confidence in union with Him.

23 – Two powerful tools

We have a powerful story in Matt 15:21-28 from which we can learn a great deal:

*²¹ **Then Jesus went out from there and departed to the region of Tyre and Sidon.** ²² **And behold, a woman of Canaan came from that region and cried out to Him, saying, "Have mercy on me, O Lord, Son of David! My daughter is severely demon-possessed."***

*²³ **But He answered her not a word. And His disciples came and urged Him, saying, "Send her away, for she cries out after us."***

*²⁴ **But He answered and said, "I was not sent except to the lost sheep of the house of Israel."** ²⁵ **Then she came and worshiped Him, saying, "Lord, help me!"***

*²⁶ **But He answered and said, "It is not good to take the children's bread and throw it to the little dogs."***

*²⁷ **And she said, "Yes, Lord, yet even the little dogs eat the crumbs which fall from their masters' table."***

28 *Then Jesus answered and said to her, "O woman, great is your faith! Let it be to you as you desire." And her daughter was healed from that very hour.*

What an unusual situation after we have been looking at God's heart which is disposed to heal! You can't have it more discouraging than this woman had it! She simply came to Jesus to ask for the healing of her daughter. What was the answer? There wasn't any at all! This was worse than a 'no'. Jesus (who was God) didn't answer. He totally ignored the woman. It's bad to be ignored by your friends or parents, but if you are ignored by God then you have a big problem. Now it gets worse. Not only did Jesus refuse to answer, but his disciples encouraged Jesus in front of the woman to get rid of her. Literally everything was contrary to what the woman had imagined. Most of us would come to the conclusion that 'it's obvious this request is not the will of God!' And that conclusion would make us give up the battle. If God said, 'No' then 'who am I to continue?' would be the conclusion reached by most of us. But not the woman of Canaan! I like that woman! She had a healthy stubbornness. Notice now the two means she used in that battle for her daughter.

It was <u>perseverance</u> and <u>humility</u>. She continued with much perseverance after all the discouragements she had received. Then she progressed from being ignored to a <u>seeming</u> refusal from Jesus. At least now she heard a reply: *"I was not sent except to the lost sheep of the house of Israel."* Did that move the woman? Not a bit! It was then that she used a second very effective means at her disposal called 'humility'. She was a very humble mum as her instant reaction of worshipping Jesus indicated – ***then she came and worshiped Him, saying, "Lord, help me!"***. She asked for help with a worshipping attitude. Would we have felt like carrying out a worshipping act in that moment of time? Next, she heard herself to being identified with a dog. Her humble spirit did not get offended. In other words, Jesus explained to her that healing and deliverance is for the Jews only. The woman however, full of faith, pointed out that crumbs are eaten by dogs. She couldn't humble herself more than that. This was the turning point. After that everything took on a new dimension. The same divine person who ignored her to begin with now says: *"O woman, great is your faith! Let it be to you as you desire."* What a mighty victory and turn around! In that moment something mighty happened in her house. The daughter was healed. The woman walked away with real assurance through the use of much perseverance and humility to achieve the healing.

The question can now be raised: did God change His mind by first saying 'no' and then 'yes'? God did not change His mind. James 5:12 says: ***"But let your "Yes" be "Yes," and your "No," "No," lest you fall into judgment."*** Jesus never said 'no' in the first place, but it would have been easy to interpret it as a 'no' because of our adopted theology, pride or lack of perseverance. In the wake of the cross healing and deliverance are now not only for the Jews but for the Gentiles also. That means, if the Syrophonecian woman received healing for her daughter when legally she had no right before the cross, how much more for us also today in the wake of the cross.

God loves persistent people. This is confirmed in the use Jesus makes of an illustration in Luke 11:5-8:

> *'And He said to them, "Which of you shall have a friend, and go to him at midnight and say to him, 'Friend, lend me three loaves; 'for a friend of mine has come to me on his journey, and I have nothing to set before him'; "and he will answer from within and say, 'Do not trouble me; the door is now shut, and my children are with me in bed; I cannot rise and give to you'? "I say to you, though he will not rise and give to him because he is his friend, yet because of his <u>persistence</u> he will rise and give him as many as he needs.' (emphasis mine)*

I remember praying for someone many times and nothing happened. It got a bit awkward as I kept asking if I could pray for him again. He hesitantly allowed me to go ahead with my prayer probably thinking though if nothing happened all these previous times then one more prayer wouldn't make any difference either. However, when I prayed 'again' an immediate change took place. Sometimes persistence pays off.

24 – Having faith on behalf of someone else

There is another noteworthy lesson for us in the story of the woman from Canaan. What exactly did she say to Jesus when she asked for healing for her daughter? She said: *"Have mercy on me, O Lord, Son of David!"* The woman was not sick but the daughter was, and yet she said *"Have mercy on me."* (emphasis mine) We can come to God and act on behalf of others. Her daughter's pain became her pain. Many times, people in need cannot or are not able to pray for themselves when it comes to healing and deliverance. Children especially fall into this category.

This situation confirms that we can have faith on behalf of someone else. The woman had faith on behalf of her daughter. Matt 15:28 says: *'Then Jesus answered and said to her, "O woman, great is your faith!"* That referred to the mum's faith and not the daughter's faith. There are more accounts in the Bible which teach us this principle. For example, when the four men were carrying their paralytic friend on a stretcher to Jesus. It clearly says *"When Jesus saw their faith".* (Mark 2:5) *(emphasis mine)* It wasn't the sick person's faith but the friends' faith. The four men had faith for the lame friend. A more obvious instance however is that in evidence when Jesus raised Lazarus from the dead. Whose faith was in view? Of course not Lazarus' faith, as he was dead. It was Jesus' faith (John 11:43).

This shows us that we are under no circumstances to blame the sick person's faith when he/she doesn't receive his/her healing. So many times, sick people are blamed for their unbelief which makes me personally sad. Yes, of course if the sick person has faith then the healing is likely to happen. I remember a situation when I prayed for a woman and she received her healing immediately, I know at the time whose faith it was. Not mine. If both believe, even better. I personally expect the one who prays for the sick person to assume a more responsible attitude. With that I don't mean if the healing doesn't take place, the praying person needs to blame himself. If it doesn't happen, we throw the emotional burden on Jesus, but we do not blame the sick person for it. When nothing happened when I prayed several times for someone, I pointed out that if Jesus had been there the sick person would have been healed. With that statement I clearly indicated that it was still the will of God for him to be made well. My lack of faith came in the way. I didn't come to the conclusion that God wanted that person to stay sick neither did I blame myself that the miracle did not take place. In reality we are learning and growing together.

This account also teaches us that in the spiritual realm, faith, healing and deliverance are not restricted by distance.

25 – How to pray for healing

It is very important to know that Jesus never prayed to the Father in the following way: 'please heal this man', or 'please free this woman from her demon'. He always gave a command to the demon to leave or spoke directly to the sickness or the sick person. We need to learn from Jesus our great example in everything in life and do the same. Some people use another principle used by Jesus and just thank God for the healing, referring to His accomplished work. There is no pattern prayer, but just to give you an example to get you started: "In Jesus' name stomach pain leave and digestion system be totally restored. I let the healing power of Jesus Christ flow into the stomach now and declare the whole digestion system to be completely healed by the blood of Jesus Christ." Or you can simply speak out the truth over the stomach saying: "by Jesus' stripes this stomach is completely healed and the digestion system is starting to work again 100% correctly. I thank you LORD that you have paid for this stomach to be healed by your blood". You basically command the sickness or pain to go and the cause of it to be healed and restored by a command speaking directly to the problem or by thanking God for the result which you clearly define, applying the truth from Isa 53:5 *'by His stripes we are healed'* or other healing Scriptures.

If God gave you an order to do something then you would not need to ask Him to do the job, because He gave the job to you. That means we shouldn't give the job back to God. You can ask God to help you and to equip you, that's totally different. The Bible says in Matt 10:7-8 **'And as you go, preach, saying, 'The kingdom of heaven is at hand.' Heal the sick, cleanse the lepers, raise the dead, cast out demons. Freely you have received, freely give.'** If we have freely received, that means we have not worked for it in prayer or in another way. It was free. If you pray for the sick with that attitude then your basis for the healing relies 100% on what Jesus has done and therefore that person may likely be healed. Never rely on how holy you are or how much you have prayed and fasted, etc. Jesus' stripes are what you rely on. After Peter and John prayed for the lame they said *'why look so intently at us, <u>as though by our own power or godliness</u> we had made this man walk?'* (Acts 3:12) (emphasis mine) We never rely on our own godliness or any form of merit, but 100% on what Jesus paid for. It has nothing really to do with us, it just so happens that God has chosen us as the instrument in His hand.

26 – The most important aspect of the healing ministry is love

The chapter of 1 Cor 13 ends with these powerful verses: *'And now abide faith, hope, love, these three; but the greatest of these is love.'* We know of course that this refers to every aspect of our Christian life, but sometimes forget that this also refers very much to the deliverance and healing ministry. I would go as far as to say that 'being led by love' is more important than the result of our healing prayer. Gal 5:6 explains that 'faith is working through love.' It's amazing that the Word of God connects faith with love. We also know that 'love your neighbour' is the second most important commandment. Let's always make love the motive of our deliverance and healing prayer as our priority. *'Love never fails.'* (1 Cor 13:8) even if the sick person remains sick.

Love is like an engine, if you are driven by it, you can go so much further than without it. I have had cases where I fought in prayer for a long time for people and I would have given up if love wasn't my motive. Especially when you minister to *people* you don't know and you may have no emotional connection to that person, then it's important to be filled with the divine love of the Holy Spirit.

> *'Now I beg you, brethren, through the Lord Jesus Christ, and through the <u>love of the Spirit</u>, that you strive together with me in prayers to God for me.' (Rom 15:30) (emphasis mine)*

These are precious people made in the image of God and loved by our Heavenly Father! We want to care for them. If we were them, then we also would love someone to minister to us in love and not treat us just as a number.

In Matt 25:36 Jesus refers to a future event when HE will declare the following words: **"I was sick and you visited Me."** What does that mean in our context? This clearly assures us that even if the person we have prayed for didn't receive his/her healing we are not condemned for the lack of our faith, but commended by Jesus Himself that we cared for that person in love.

27 – We are ambassadors in this world

An ambassador is an authorized representative of his own country in another country. He lives in that foreign country and represents his own government. Ambassadors are appointed for specific tasks and have a temporary mission. This is exactly the job description of every Christian! We are authorized by Jesus Himself and we are appointed to different tasks. We read: *"Go therefore and make disciples of all nations"* (Matt 28:19) An ambassador's mission and task is to make disciples. Sometimes a lot of things need to happen before someone becomes a disciple, like preaching the gospel in love, setting them free and ministering healing to them. All these steps are leading to the end goal which is 'making disciples'. We are basically reconciling the people of a foreign country we live in called 'the world' with the country 'Heaven' to which we belong. 2 Cor 5:19 says: *'And has committed to us the word of reconciliation.'* This is a temporary task and it lasts only as long as we live in this foreign country. Our real home is Heaven. Jesus says about his children: *"They are not of the world, just as I am not of the world."* John 17:14

All born-again Christians are true ambassadors and need to take their mission very seriously. This is a highly prioritised and urgent task! The Bible says *"We are ambassadors for Christ, as though God were pleading through us: we implore you on Christ's behalf, be reconciled to God."* (2 Cor 5:20)

Every ambassador also needs to make sure that he represents Jesus morally and doctrinally. He always needs to be on guard for every aspect in his life. Seeking holiness and becoming more like Jesus is a major part of this (*'Pursue peace with all people, and holiness, without which no one will see the Lord.'* Heb 12:14) This is of course only possible through the power of the Holy Spirit, otherwise we are trying to please God in the flesh which can become a religious exercise. If we practise the second command (**'You shall love your neighbour as yourself.'** Matt 22:39) and have love and compassion in our hearts we are good ambassadors. If we struggle in this area then sincerely pray to God to give you love and compassion through the Holy Spirit

Heavenly ambassadors are never alone! Jesus promised to every ambassador that He will always be with them in that foreign country until at last they are called up to their Heavenly Home (**'And lo, I am with you always even unto the end of the age.'** Matt 28:20)

When you are involved in deliverance and healing then always be aware of the fact that Jesus is literally with you. You have His authority to do that job as He is the one who has appointed you for it in the first place.

28 – Final words about healing

In view of all that has been said – where do doctors and medication come into all this? People sometimes are not sure if they act in unbelief when they take medication. First of all, thank God for doctors! I believe you can take medication and rely on God at the same time and not compromise. People have died, because they stopped taking medication as an act of faith. Let the Holy Spirit work. When you pray for healing or someone prays for you, then stop the medication when your healing is confirmed. And you can even go to the doctor to get it confirmed. It's that simple. I'm not saying that there is no place to stop taking medicine in faith. We need to let the Holy Spirit work this out, but never be foolish in the process! If no healing is activated, then it's better to keep taking medicine and use the time to grow in faith and receive divine healing later, rather than dying in a well-meant faith!
In closing, remember God's Word is the plumb line, not our experience. I hope this helps you to feel totally at ease and free to pray for the sick without any hesitations, and to grow in faith.

David Ohin

CHAPTER 9

Final words

29 – Final words

Setting somebody free can sometimes be like peeling each layer off an onion until everything is removed. Some things may take longer and some can be dealt with very quickly. This is one reason why I would appeal to the body of Christ to seek the gifts of **'discerning of spirits'** *(1 Cor 12:10)* **and 'the word of knowledge'** (1 Cor 12:8) which can speed up the process of deliverance and inner healing considerably. It also makes it much easier. In addition, it is a huge safeguard against all the deception which can be expected to increase these last days.

I have heard of someone I ministered to, who told me that she had been in several Christian gatherings where literally a satanic spirit was operating by one so-called "Christian". That person was a "plant" of the enemy and was involved in the occult and when he laid hands on people and prayed, the person they were praying for became demonized. Nobody suspected that this was so until much damage had been done to people, and even then, many did not believe it was possible for Christians to be affected this way. This was one of the reasons she came to me for deliverance.

My advice is to stick as closely to the Word of God as you can. This is our light, our security and the ultimate safeguard! *('Your word is a lamp to my feet and a light to my path.'* Psa 119:105).

30 – Conclusion

The most effective way in the deliverance ministry is not only to ensure spiritual freedom for people but to remove every legal entry point and deal with the issues of the heart, which is the root of the entry point. Once a person is truly free, it's very important to explain to that person that it's not just about feeling better and enjoying a life of freedom but to inherit the destiny that God intends for you. Eph 2:10 teaches us: **'For we are His workmanship, created in Christ Jesus for good works, which God prepared beforehand that we should walk in them.'** God created every human being for a specific purpose and He wants us to pursue His original plans for our lives. Once you are free from bondages, curses and demons, you can grow in God's purposes. When you do that, you have not only found the keys of freedom but can also enjoy a truly satisfying and happy life.

31 - Making Jesus Lord

If you now understand the big battle which is going on in this world and you realise that you are still on the wrong side, then now is the appropriate time in your life to change sides, in leaving the prince of this world (satan) and making Jesus King in your life; the One who has paid for your sin on the cross with His own blood in order to cleanse you from ALL the sins you have ever committed and saved you for eternity. Through His blood, all the eternal consequences and applications of your past sins will be destroyed and made null (**'To Him who loved us and washed us from our sins in His own blood…'** Rev 1:5). If you want that, then pray something like the following prayer with all your heart and Jesus will save you instantly:

Lord Jesus Christ, I know I have sinned in my thoughts, words and actions. There are so many good things I have not done. There are so many sinful things I have done.

I have…(eg. been angry, selfish, told lies, sexual sins, betrayed, hurt etc.) I am truly sorry for my sins and I want to turn from everything I know to be wrong.

I realize that my sins have separated me from You. Please forgive me and cleanse me from all my sins. You gave your life upon the cross for me. Gratefully I give my life to you.

Now I ask you to come into my life as my personal Saviour. Come in as my Lord and make me Your child. From now on I want to follow You and make you the King of my life.

I put my full trust in You and Your righteousness only and not anymore in all the good works and deeds I have done.

I thank You from the bottom of my heart that You have saved and forgiven me. AMEN!

List of occultic terms:

Before you go through this list, I would like to point out that each item is on a different scale in terms of danger and harm. Like there are different snakes, some are very poisonous and you die pretty much straightaway and others are less poisonous, yet you still get harmed greatly. The fact is, if one bites you, then you are bitten. I would highly recommend to stay away from all of them, all the time!

(This list is by no means complete.)

Acupuncture, alchemy, amulets, ankh, apotropaion, apparitions, astral projection, astral plane, astrology, augury, aura, automatic writing, avatar, birth signs, birth stones, black arts, black magic, black mass, blood subscription, cartomancy, chain letters, chakra, channelling, charm, clairaudience, clairsentience, clairvoyance, cleromancy, colour therapy, conjuration, coven, crystal ball gazing, crystals for healing, curse, death magic, déjà vu (thinking you have seen or experienced a situation or place before, even though it's physically impossible), demon worship, divination, divining rod, dowsing, druid, ectoplasm, enchanting, evil eye, extrasensory perception, fetish, fire-walking, folk charm, fortune-telling, grimoires (a book of magic spells and invocations), guided imagery, heavy metal rock music, hepatoscopy, hex, hexagram, homeopathy, horoscopes, horse brasses, hydromancy, hypnotism, idols, incubus, iridology, jinx, juju, kabbalah, karma, levitation, ley lines, libation, literomancy, lucky charms, charm bracelets, magician, mandala, mantra, martial arts, medium, mesmerism, mind control, metaphysics, mindfulness, mind reading, mind science, mojo, moonmancy, mother earth beliefs, mother goddess beliefs, motorskopua, mysticism, necromancy, neopagan, new age, new age symbols, numerology, Obeah or Obi, occult literature, occult symbols, om, omens, Ouija board, palmistry, pantheism belief, parakinesis, parapsychology, pendulum, pentacle, pentagram, phrenology, physiognomy, planchette, poltergeist, polytheism belief, precognition, premonition, psychic birth, psychic healing, psychic sight, psychometry, punk rock, pyramidology, reflexology, Reiki healing, reincarnation, remote viewing, rolfing, satanism, scrying, séances, shaman, shape shifting, sorcery, soul travel, spell, spirit guide, spiritism (spiritualism), stang, stigmata, superstitions, sympathetic magic, table tipping, talisman, Tantra, tarot, tea-leaf reading, telekinesis, telepathy, therapeutic touch, theurgy, third eye, trance, transcendental meditation, translocation, transmigration, voodoo, wand or blasting rod, white magic, wicca, witchcraft, yoga, zodiac.

List of some alternative medical practices with potential danger:

Here again I would like to give some thoughts before you go through these terms. Many remedies and its principles are originally God given for the well-being and healing of humans. They are good and not dangerous at all. The enemy has known that and taken advantage of it by distorting the original remedies attaching a dangerous spiritual implication to it in order to pursue his goals which we have discussed in this book. That means some of the following terms can be really helpful if they are totally separated from their spiritual practices. However, the majority cannot be separated from the spiritual implications and therefore are dangerous. I would highly recommend for you to stay away from them to ensure your personal safety and security.

I give you an example of a milder form of danger:

Two elderly devoted Christian women, who had great difficulty in their prayer lives were apparently healed by homeopathic medicine. Later it was discovered that the two ladies had received exactly the same medicine from a medical practitioner beforehand. But that medicine didn't work at all. It was obvious that it wasn't the medicine, which helped them, but the spiritual application behind it. The two women repented and asked Jesus to forgive them. After that, God delivered them and all the difficulties they experienced were gone.

(A German doctor Samuel Ch.F. Hahnemann was the founder of homeopathy. He believed he received the knowledge of it by a revelation from heavenly powers. One of the prominent homeopaths declared openly that only 3% is based on natural medicine.)

(This list is by no means complete.)

Acupressure, Acupuncture, Allopathy, Aromatherapy (the natural oils in themselves are not the problem, it's when they are used in the context of the aromatherapy original thoughts of the balance of harmony between body and mind or when you submit to an Aromatherapist), Attachment therapy, Aura-soma, Autogenic training and autosuggestion, Ayurveda, Bach flower remedies, Bates method, Chelation therapy, Chinese medicine, Christian Science, Colour therapy or chromotherapy, Crystal therapy, Faith healers (Non-Christian), Flower essence therapy, Guided imagery, Herbalism, Herbology, Homeopathy, Hypnotherapy, Iridology, Jin Shin Jyutsu, Macrobiotic lifestyle, Magnetic healing, Medical intuition, Meditation (of course we refer to Non-Christian meditation), Naturopathic medicine, New Age medicine, Past lives therapy, Polarity therapy, Psychic healers Psychic surgery, Pyramid healing, Qigong, Quantum-touch, Radiesthesia, Rebirthing, Reflexology, Reiki, Rolfing, Shiatsu, Sophrology, Spiritualist healing, Tantra, Therapeutic touch, Some Traditional Chinese medicine.

David Ohin

For more information contact:

David Ohin
C/O Advantage Books
P.O. Box 160847
Altamonte Springs, FL 32716
info@advbooks.com

To purchase additional copies of these books, visit our bookstore at:
www.advbookstore.com

Longwood, Florida, USA
"we bring dreams to life"™
www.advbookstore.com

www.ingramcontent.com/pod-product-compliance
Lightning Source LLC
Chambersburg PA
CBHW061455040426
42450CB00007B/1366